The Literary Remains Of Lady Jane Grey: With A Memoir Of Her Life

Jane Grey

THE
LITERARY REMAINS

OF

LADY JANE GREY;

WITH

A Memoir of her Life.

BY NICHOLAS HARRIS NICOLAS, ESQ.

FELLOW OF THE SOCIETY OF ANTIQUARIES.

In hire is high beaute withouten pride,
Youthe, withouten grenehed or folie:
To all hire werkes vertue is hire guide;
Humblesse hath slaien in hire tyrannie:
She is a mirrour of alle curtesie,
Hire herte is veray chambre of holinesse,
Hire hond ministre of fredom for almesse.

Chaucer.

LONDON:

PUBLISHED BY HARDING, TRIPHOOK, AND LEPARD,
FINSBURY SQUARE.

MDCCCXXV.

PREFACE.

AT a period when reprints of the works of early writers are daily issuing from the press, it is not a little extraordinary that a perfect collection of the literary productions of LADY JANE GREY should never have appeared; nor is this neglect justified either by the obscurity of the author, or by their own want of merit. The name of that illustrious female is well known to the world, and were there nothing but her royal birth, her youth, and beauty, and a most eventful life to excite interest, her lucubrations would possess high, though melancholy claims to attention; but with respect to the pieces themselves, it is merely requisite to observe, that when compared with the writings of her contemporaries, their literary excellence appears in so strong a light, that a doubt is created whether they could possibly have been the compositions of a girl under seventeen years of age. Her peculiar situation, together with other circumstances, tend, however, to con-

vince us of their authenticity, and one of them
exists at the present day in her own manuscript.

In the memoir which is prefixed to this
volume, an account is given of her life, hence
it is only necessary in this place to offer some
observations on the articles which are attributed
to her pen. The following list comprises what
are considered to have been unquestionably
written by herself.

Three letters in Latin to Henry Bullinger. These
    letters were written before her marriage, and
    between the years 1550 and 1553. Transla-
    tions of them are also inserted.

A letter to a friend newly fallen from the Faith.
    This letter is said to have been addressed to
    Dr. Hardinge, but as it was certainly written
    before her marriage, and as he did not declare
    his apostacy until after the accession of
    Mary, the assertion, as is more fully observed
    in the following memoir, is probably erro-
    neous, unless she was informed of his senti-
    ments before he publicly avowed them.

*A Conference with Feckenham, Queen Mary's
    Chaplain;* written in February, 1554, a few
    days before her execution.

*A Prayer for her own use whilst a Prisoner in the
    Tower.* As Lady Jane Grey was committed

to the Tower in July, 1553, and executed on the 12 February, 1554, it must have been composed within that period.

A letter to her Father, also written in the Tower, and probably, only a few weeks before her death.

A letter to her Sister Katherine. This letter was written Sunday, 11 February, 1554, the night before her execution, in a blank leaf of a Greek New Testament.

Notes, &c. in a MS. Manual of Prayers. As the Duke of Suffolk, to whom two of these notes were addressed, was not committed to the Tower until the 10th February, they must have been written within two days of her decease. This MS. with the notes in question, is now in the British Museum.

All of the preceding are reprinted in this volume, as are also some *Latin lines*, said to have been written by her on the walls of her prison with a pin; but it is by no means certain that they are genuine, for no trace of them existed when the other inscriptions in the Tower were discovered. As, however, they have been constantly ascribed to her, and as they do not contain any internal evidence to the contrary, it was not thought advisable to omit them. Lord Orford states, that Lady Jane Grey likewise wrote two pieces, the one, entitled *The Duty of a Christian,* and the other *The Complaint of a Sinner,* but after a diligent enquiry, neither of them could be found; nor does his Lordship inform us where they exist. In all probability these titles were other names for articles printed in this collection under different appellations. *The Duty of a Christian* well describes what is generally styled *Her conference with Feckenham,* which commences with the interrogation of "What thing is required in a Christian;" and the *Complaint of a Sinner* might be used to designate *The Prayer composed for her own use.* Hollingshed and Baker assert, that she wrote "other things," but neither of these Chroniclers specify or refer to them; and as no other of her productions, excepting "Three Epigrams on her Husband's Body, one in English, one in Greek, and the third in Latin," is noticed by either of her numerous biographers, it may be concluded, whatever else she might have written, that nothing besides what is collected in this volume has been preserved. The "Epigrams" alluded to, it is contended in the following pages, were never written by Lady Jane Grey.

On the subject of her works it must be further remarked, that this collection contains every thing which is known to be extant; and in the narrative of her life some observations on their authenticity, and the period when, as well as the circumstances under which they were composed, are introduced. It will be seen that Religion was the chief subject that employed her pen; and whilst the situation in which from her childhood she had the misfortune to be placed, accounts for the selection of so solemn a theme, her virtues and unmerited sorrows, bestow on her productions a deep and permanent interest. Purer morality or more important precepts were never expressed; and at the same time, that the writings of this admirable young woman, are, from the period in which she lived, and the proofs which they afford of her extraordinary attainments, literary curiosities, the filial devotion, resignation, and piety they display, entitle them to the highest commendation.

The MEMOIR OF LADY JANE GREY has been drawn up from the best authorities; and

the most valuable of the state papers relating to
her usurpation are inserted. No documents
hitherto inedited could be discovered which were
in any degree connected with her life, nor is it
pretended that many new facts are developed:
yet as the statements of former writers have been
carefully collated, by which some erroneous conclusions have been detected, and as the historical
question of her claim to the throne is not only
fully discussed, but is illustrated by an extensive
genealogical table——which exhibits the succession of every monarch of this kingdom from
the reign of Edward the Fourth; the pretensions
of the personages to whom, by the will of Henry
the Eighth, the crown was limited; together
with the descent of the present representative of
Lady Jane Grey——it is hoped that the original
matter in this volume will be deemed worthy of
notice, not merely by the admirers of that celebrated woman, but also by those who are interested in that part of English History in which
she was so unfortunately involved.

August, 1825.

MEMOIR

OF

LADY JANE GREY.

———

Perhaps no character has ever been pourtrayed which excites the noble feelings of the human heart in so powerful a degree, as that of the unfortunate Lady Jane Grey; nor would it be possible to select a more perfect example of those virtues which adorn the female bosom, and confer dignity upon the most elevated rank, than is exhibited in her writings and conduct. But though possessed of every claim to admiration, such was the inscrutable will of that Being, to whose fiat no one could be more disposed to submit than herself, that her brief existence was not only embittered by unusual and almost constant misfortunes, but it was terminated by a violent, and in the eye of moral justice, an unmerited death.

Notwithstanding that she scarcely attained her seventeenth year, few personages have filled so important a part in the political transactions of their times, and whilst an object of the deepest interest to every mind capable of being affected

b

by the romantic events of her life, all which relates to her is of the greatest importance to the historian. For these reasons numerous accounts of this illustrious female have been given to the public; indeed, so many authors have made her the subject of their pens, that in this sketch of her character little hope is entertained of presenting new facts; but although every expectation of displaying traits, or recording events hitherto unnoticed, is disclaimed, this memoir may nevertheless not be totally unworthy of attention, from the consideration that the same data frequently admit of different conclusions.

If lineage to a mind so well regulated as Lady Jane Grey's could confer pride, she had a sufficient cause for it in the contemplation of her ancestry. Her father's family was one of the oldest in the kingdom, and had in several branches been ennobled; Rollo, or Fulbert, is said to have been Chamberlain to Robert, Duke of Normandy, and to have obtained from that Prince the castle of Croy, in Picardy; from which territory he adopted the surname of De Croy, afterwards altered to De Grey: according to many writers, his grandson Sir Arnold de Grey, accompanied William the Conqueror into England, and was seated at Rotherfield, in the county of Oxford, soon after the conquest: but the first of the family noticed by

Dugdale,[a] is Henry de Grey, who obtained from
Richard I. a grant of the manor of Thurrock, in
Essex, and which was confirmed to him by King
John, in the first year of his reign, with an ad-
ditional charter of license to hunt the hare and fox
in any lands belonging to the crown, excepting in
the King's own demesne parks: from the younger
sons of this Henry have sprung the numerous families of Grey, whose names are so conspicuous
in the Baronage and History of England. John,
the second son, was justice of Chester in 1248,
33 Henry III., and was the father of Reginald de
Grey, who also became justice of Chester, and for
his eminent services received a grant from Edward
I. of the castle of Ruthyn, and in the twenty-third
year of that monarch's reign was summoned to
parliament: dying in 1308, he was succeeded in
his honours by John, his son and heir, who was
twice married; the issue by his first wife continued
the baronial line of Grey de Wilton, which existed
in uninterrupted descent and honor for above three
centuries, when the male line not only failed, but
the dignities of that house were forfeited by the
attainder of Thomas Lord Grey of Wilton, in 1614.
By his second wife, Maud, daughter of Ralph,
Lord Basset of Drayton, John Lord Grey, had a

---

[a] *Baronage,* tome i. p. 709.

younger son, Roger, on whom he bestowed the
castle and lands of Ruthyn, and who founded a
house equal in splendour and reputation to that
of Grey of Wilton; he was summoned to Parliament as Lord Grey of Ruthyn, in the 17th of
Edward II., and died on the 6th of March, 1353,
leaving Reginald his second son his heir, as John
de Grey the eldest, who was a personage of considerable consequence, died in the life time of his
father. Reginald, second Lord Grey of Ruthyn,
in common with the other nobility of that age,
served in the wars of France, and died in 1388,
when Reginald his son and heir inherited his father's
dignities, and was a very distinguished baron in the
latter part of the reign of Richard II., and under
Henry IV. and Henry V. He married two wives;
by Mary, the first, he had Sir John de Grey, who
died before his father, and left Edmund de Grey,
his son and heir, who succeeded his grandfather in
his honours, and was created earl of Kent by
Edward IV., and from whom the earls of Kent,
and barons Grey de Ruthyn derived their descent.
Reginald, third Lord Grey of Ruthyn, married,
secondly, Joan, daughter and heiress of William,
Lord Astley, and by her had three sons, the two
youngest of which founded houses of considerable
provincial distinction, but were never ennobled,
and the eldest son, Sir Edward de Grey, was the

immediate ancestor of the subject of this memoir,
and the founder of a family that attained more
elevated honors than either of the other branches.
Sir Edward de Grey married Elizabeth, daughter
and heir of Henry Ferrers, who died in his father's
life time, the eldest son of William, Lord Ferrers
of Groby, and she being heir to that barony, her
husband was in her right summoned to Parliament,
as Lord Ferrers of Groby, in 1448. A curious
record which is extant relative to this baron and
his wife, is worthy of notice, as being in some
degree illustrative of the manners of the times.
Groby in Leicestershire, the residence of this
noble pair, was situated at a considerable distance
from the parish church, the obstacles to reaching which were much increased by the badness of
the roads. In 1446, Lady Grey, or more properly speaking, Lady Ferrers of Groby, being
near her confinement, and the customs of the age
requiring that a child should be baptized immediately after its birth, her husband obtained a
license from John Stafford, then archbishop of
Canterbury, dated at Lambeth, 8th November,
1446, that "in respect of the great distance of
his manor-house of Groby from the parish church,
and the foulness of the ways thereto, he might
christen that child at his said house, by the Vicar
of his chapel, wherewith Dame Elizabeth his wife

was then great and near the time of her delivery." [a]
Lord Ferrers of Groby died December 18th, 1460,
when the barony devolved on John de Grey, his
son and heir, who married the famous Elizabeth
Woodville, daughter of Sir Richard Woodville,
who was afterwards created Earl Rivers; her husband being slain at the battle of St. Alban's, she
was left a widow with two sons, Sir Thomas, and
Sir Richard Grey, in whose favour she became a
suitor to King Edward IV., when that monarch,
deeply struck with her beauty, which was naturally
heightened by that interest which is uniformly
created by loveliness in misfortune, soon afterwards
rendered her the partner of his throne. It is a
fact rendered trite by repetition, that an alliance
with royalty has ever been attended with the loss
of happiness, and frequently with that of life; the
fate of Lady Jane Grey, as well as that of her
family, not only affords a melancholy confirmation
of the assertion, but another instance is to be
found in the misery which attended the last years
of the interesting Elizabeth Woodville. Much as
has been written about this celebrated woman, a
document under her own hand appears to have es-
caped general notice, and this circumstance, united
to the consideration of her being the great-great-

[a] Dugdale's *Baronage*, tome i. p. 719.

grandmother of Lady Jane, as well as the pro-
genitress of every monarch who has ascended the
throne since the death of Richard III., will perhaps
justify its being here introduced. It is well known
that Henry VII., on pretences as absurd as they
were cruel, and which can only be attributed to
the jealousy of his disposition, seized on all his
mother-in-law's possessions, when she retired, or
as is more probable, was confined to the Abbey of
Bermondsey, in which place she died. Of her destitute condition, and the deep sense which she entertained of it, we have a most affecting memorial
in her Will, and a more plaintive record of her love
for her children, and her sorrow that she had
nothing but her blessing to bequeath to them,
could not be imagined.

"In Dei Nomine. The xth day of April,
the year of our Lord God, M.CCCC.LXXXXII. I
Elizabeth, by the grace of God, Queen of England,
late wife to the most victorious Prince of blessed
memory, Edward IV., being of whole mind; seeing
the world so transitory, and no creature certain
when they shall depart from hence, having Almighty God fresh in mind, in whom is all mercy
and grace, bequeath my soul into his hands, beseeching him of the same mercy to accept it gra-
ciously; and our blessed Lady, Queen of comfort,
and all the holy company of Heaven to be good
means for me.

" Item, I bequeath my body to be buried with
the body of my lord at Windsor, according to the
will of my said lord and mine, without pompes
entreing[a] or costly expences done thereabouts.

" Item, Whereas I have no worldly goods to do
the Queen's grace, my dearest daughter, a pleasure
with, neither to reward any of my children according to my heart and mind, I beseech Almighty
God to bless her grace with all her noble issue,
and with as good heart and mind as is to me possible, I give her grace my blessing, and all the
aforesaid my children.

" Item, I will that such small stuff and goods
that I have, be disposed truly in contentation of
my debts, and for the health of my soul, as far as
they will extend.

" Item, If any of my blood will any of my said
stuff or goods to me pertaining, I will that they
have the preferment before any other,[b] and of
this my present Testament, I make and ordain
mine executors, that is to say, John Ingilby,
Prior of the Charter House of Shene, William
Sutton, and Thomas Brent, Doctors; and I beseech my said dearest daughter, the Queen's

[a] Without a pompous Funeral.
[b] This bequest must mean, that in the event of her
kindred being desirous of possessing any of her goods, to
keep in remembrance of her, they might be allowed to
purchase it in preference to strangers.

grace, and my son Thomas, Marquess of Dorset, to put their good wills, and help for the performance of this my Testament.

"In witness whereof, to this my present Testament, I have set my seal; these witnesses, John, Abbot of Saint Saviour of Bermondsey, and Benedictus Cum, Doctor of Physick. Given the year and day aforesaid."[a]

Cold and unenviable indeed must be the heart of that person, who can peruse this affecting testimony of the once lovely Queen of England's destitution, without being moved with contempt at the author of her misfortunes, more particularly when it is remembered, that he who thus persecuted an unprotected female, was the husband of her daughter!

Thomas, Lord Grey of Groby, Queen Elizabeth's eldest son by her first husband, was created Earl of Huntingdon by his father-in-law, in 1471, but which title he soon afterwards resigned, and was created Marquess of Dorset, on the 18th April, 1475, and was also elected a Knight of the Garter; but on Edward IV.'s demise, his relationship to the young monarch rendered him an object of suspicion, and he was attainted of high treason in the first year of Richard III.: on the

---

[a] *Royal Wills*, 1780, 4to. p. 350.

accession of Henry VII. he was, however, fully
restored to his honours, and dying in 1501,
was succeeded in his dignities by his son Thomas,
second Marquess of Dorset, who was a celebrated soldier, and in that age of chivalry often
distinguished himself at jousts and tournaments;
he was also elected a Knight of the Garter, and
died in 1530.   His son and heir, Henry Grey,
inherited all his father's honors, namely, the
Marquisate of Dorset, and the Baronies of Ferrers
of Groby, Astley, Bonville, and Harington, the
two latter of which dignities were acquired by the
marriage of Thomas, the first Marquess, with
Cecily Bonville, who inherited the Barony of
Harington from her father, and that of Bonville
from her great-grandfather.

The monotonous details of genealogy must
now be succeeded by a relation of those interesting events, which produced the fall of this
illustrious house.   Henry Grey, Marquess of
Dorset, when he succeeded to the honors of his
family, may be considered, in point of rank, as
one of the most powerful noblemen of his times;
in the first year of the reign of his kinsman, Edward VI., he was constituted Lord High Constable
for that Monarch's coronation, and was elected a
Knight of the Garter; in 1550, 4 Edw. VI., he was
appointed Justice Itinerant of all the King's forests;

and in the next year Warden of the East, West, and
Middle Marshes towards Scotland; at an early
period of his life he was betrothed to Katherine
Fitz-Alan, daughter of William, Earl of Arundel, a
connection perfectly suited to his birth, and which
was sufficiently splendid to satisfy whatever aristo-
cratic feelings he might possess, without being attended with danger to himself or his posterity.
This lady is presumed to have died without issue,[a]
and he soon afterwards formed that alliance which
proved so unfortunate in its consequences, by
marrying Lady Frances Brandon, eldest daughter
of Charles Brandon, Duke of Suffolk, by Mary,
widow of Louis XII. King of France, second
daughter of King Henry VII., and youngest sister
of King Henry VIII; the character of the Marquess of Dorset appears to have been that of
a quiet unambitious man, for although some
writers have described him as not deficient either
in ambition or courage, none have attributed any
quality to him which could render him a dangerous subject, and perhaps Dugdale's remark is
not far from the truth, when he observes, that in
consequence of his marriage, and the death of his
wife's brothers without children, " he was, in fa-

[a] Some remarks on this alliance, which has been the
subject of much discussion, will be found towards the conclusion of the memoir.

vour to her, though otherwise for his harmless simplicity, neither misliked nor much regarded, created Duke of Suffolk."

Lady Jane Grey, their eldest daughter, is supposed to have been born at Bradgate, in Leicestershire, about the year 1537, and was through her mother, grand niece of Henry VIII., and consequently first cousin once removed to his son and successor Edward VI. Of her early years we have no account, nor does it appear likely that they should present subjects for biography; it is manifest that her education was carefully attended to, for her eulogists describe her as having been deeply versed in Latin, Greek, Hebrew, Chaldaic, Arabic, French, and Italian, but this assertion must be received with great caution; that she possessed acquirements, now properly deemed neither requisite nor useful in female education, cannot be doubted; but it would be absurd to attribute to her much proficiency in seven languages, when a long life would scarcely be sufficient to attain even half that number with correctness; especially as the same partial writers inform us, that she played well on musical instruments, and excelled in works of the needle. The fact probably was, that the pedantry which in that age was frequently mistaken for learning, had caused the tutors of Lady Jane to give her a slight knowledge of each of the different

languages in question, but for any purpose of
utility, it is very questionable if her knowledge
extended beyond Greek, Latin, and French.   Her
principal preceptor is said to have been John
Aylmer, afterwards Bishop of London, though her
biographers attribute part of her acquirements to
Roger Ascham.   It would be useless to follow the
example of a recent writer on the times of Lady
Jane Grey, by speculating upon what books formed
her library, or to fill up from imagination the minute circumstances in the life of a young female,
which it is impossible should be preserved for
above three hundred years, and which, if recorded,
would scarcely merit attention.   It is an error of
frequent occurrence in biography, to suppose that
the early years of those who attain celebrity must
exhibit some traits of a peculiar nature, and hence
every school-boy feat, or childish expression, which
if the individuals had remained in obscurity would
have received no more notice than it deserved,
is presented in the most vivid colours as the prog-
nostications of that genius or courage, which rendered them in after life the subject of public consideration.   Until Lady Jane was made the sacrifice of parental ambition, her life appears to have
presented no other features of superiority than
what might naturally have been expected from the
possession of a strong natural understanding, cul-

tivated and improved by a learned education, and
an innate love of letters. Her disposition, we are
informed, was peculiarly mild and unassuming, and
she was certainly early impressed with a full sense
of the duties and value of religion.

After the death of Henry VIII., in 1547, his
widow, Queen Katherine Parr, resided at Chel-
sea, and we have evidence that Lady Jane Grey
was her guest, both before and subsequent to her
Majesty's union with Lord Seymour of Sudley, the
Lord Admiral. At this time though Lady Jane had
but just attained her eleventh year, her marriage
became an object of serious consideration to those
most interested in the event, and it is an unquestionable fact, that the disposal of her hand was conceded by her parents to the Lord Admiral; the
cause of this promise can only be conjectured, but it
is evident that he placed the highest value on it,
and he appears to have been actuated by the hope
of rendering her the instrument of his ambitious
projects. In September, 1548, whilst she was
residing with the Queen Dowager at Hanworth,
her Majesty died, and it was the first intention of
Lord Seymour to send her to her own home, but he
very soon altered his resolution. In a recent life
of Lady Jane Grey,* a very curious correspond-

* *Lady Jane Grey and her Times,* by George Howard,
Esq. 8vo. p. 156.

ence is given between his Lordship and the Marquess and Marchioness of Dorset on the subject of her return, from which it is clear that Seymour was anxious to retain her, whilst her parents were naturally desirous to have her under their own roof, probably not deeming a man of the Lord Admiral's calculating, and somewhat suspicious character, the proper guardian for their daughter. From the Marquess' letter we also obtain proof of the promise having been made to Seymour relative to her marriage; for, after stating that he deemed a mother's protection and guidance of essential importance to his daughter, he adds, "my meaning herein is not to withdraw any part of my promise to you for her bestowing; for I assure your Lordship, I intend, God willing, to use your discreet advice and consent in that behalf, and no less than mine own." The address of the Marchioness' letter to Lord Seymour is rather amusing; she styles him her good brother, and herself his sister, though the only connection between them was, that the Lord Admiral's wife was the widow of the Marchioness' uncle, King Henry VIII.! The result of this correspondence was, however, Lady Jane's return to her father's mansion, but the Lord Admiral's plans did not admit of her being long from under his immediate care, and after repeated efforts to render her his guest, it may be inferred that he

actually bribed her father to part with her. This
singular fact is placed beyond controversy by a
paper, cited by Mr. Howard,[a] written by the Marquess of Dorset himself, after the Lord Admiral's[b]
trial, wherein he states that it was his determination
not to have permitted her to return to Seymour, but
that the Lord Admiral went himself to Dorset
House, "and was so earnest in persuasion, that he
could not resist him, amongst the which persuasions was that he would marry her to the King's
Majesty," and lest an opposition might be caused by
the Marchioness, Sir William Skerington was employed by Seymour to overcome her reluctance.
The most curious part of the transaction is the
bribe alluded to, and though the fact is stated by the
author just quoted, he does not seem to have viewed
it in this light. We are informed that Lady Jane
returned to Hanworth, when Seymour immediately
sent her father 500l. "as it were for an earnest

[a] *Lady Jane Grey and her Times*, p. 161.

[b] Mr. Howard, in common with most other writers,
erroneously speaks of the Lord Admiral as Lord Sudley;
his proper designation was Lord Seymour of Sudley, he
having been created Baron Seymour of Sudley, in the
county of Gloucester, on the 16th February, 1547. The
error is as great as it would be to call Lord Ducie, Lord
Tortworth, because that nobleman is Baron Ducie of Tortworth, in the county of Gloucester.

penny of the favor that he would shew unto him, and which sum formed part of 2000*l.* that he had promised to lend him, and for which he refused any bond, saying that the Lady Jane should be his pledge!" These facts being admitted by the Marquess of Dorset, no other conclusion can be drawn, than that when all other means of persuasion failed, Seymour took advantage of his pecuniary wants, and promised to lend him the large sum above mentioned; but it appears that no part of the money was to be paid until he had the object of his solicitude in his own hands, and then a fourth part only was produced.

In 1549 Lord Seymour was beheaded, and it is not quite certain whether the allusion noticed by Mr. Howard in a letter from the Marquess of Dorset to the Duke of Somerset, relative to a projected alliance between Lady Jane and the Earl of Hertford, the Duke's son, was before or after that event; but the very cautious manner in which he speaks of it, " Item, for the marriage of your Grace's son to be had with my daughter Jane, I think it not meet to be written, but I shall at all times avouch my saying," favours the belief that it was during his life-time. It appears a point however of some doubt, whether, notwithstanding the jealousy which existed on the part of the Lord Admiral towards his brother the Protector, the

plan of strengthening the influence of their family,
by marrying Lady Jane to Lord Hertford, was not
the motive of Seymour's exertions to keep her in
his power; for as he had no children, nor any
nearer relation eligible in point of years to be her
husband, we cannot account for the extraordinary
interest he evinced about her marriage, unless we
imagine that in the event of his views relative to the
Princess Elizabeth failing, he himself contemplated
making her his wife. The former of these conjectures is supported by the fact, that at the time
when he displayed such anxiety about Lady Jane
Grey he had become reconciled to his brother; and
the latter, by the recollection that as the disparity
of years between him and the Princess Elizabeth
formed no obstacle to his ambitious plans, he
would not have deemed the slight difference of
four years between her age and that of Lady
Jane an impediment, had his interest tended to
make a union with her desirable. At this distance of time it must be useless to investigate
the subject, and the probable conclusion to be
drawn from the conduct of the Lord Admiral in
relation to Lady Jane Grey is, that he was merely
anxious to obtain the power of disposing of her
when she became of a marriageable age, in such a
manner as would best advance his views or support
his interest, without at that time being determined

whether he should espouse her, or whether she
should become the wife of his nephew, or of
some other nobleman on whom he could depend.

Such, in all probability, were the speculations
relative to this amiable girl in her childhood, and
who even at that early period of her life seemed
destined to be the victim of ambition. At no
period of our history was the detestable disposition
to render every connection subservient to political
purposes so much the prevailing feeling, as in the
reigns of the Tudors; the ties of friendship or of
kindred were seldom suffered to interfere, when
opposed to the prospect of advancement; self interest superseded every other consideration, and
little as honesty and generosity are to be looked
for in courtiers, the total absence of these virtues
was never so manifested as when that dynasty
swayed the English sceptre. In 1551, Roger
Ascham, Lady Jane's early tutor, visited her at
Bradgate, previous to his departure for Germany,
and his account of the interview affords interesting
information of her pursuits and disposition: he
states, that on his arrival he found that the Marquess
and Marchioness of Dorset, with their attendants,
were hunting in the park, and that Lady Jane was
in her chamber reading the Phædo of Plato, in
Greek; and to his inquiry why she did not join in
the amusement in which her family were engaged,

she replied with a smile, "I wisse [think] all
their sport in the park is but a shadow to that pleasure that I find in Plato—alas, good folk, they never
felt what true pleasure means." Ascham then en-
quired, "and how came you, madam, to this deep
knowledge of pleasure, and what did chiefly allure
you unto it, seeing not many women, but very few
men have attained thereunto?"—"I will tell you,"
she replied, "and tell you a truth, which per-
chance you will marvel at. One of the greatest
benefits that ever God gave me, is that he sent me
so sharp and severe parents, and so gentle a school-
master, for when I am in presence either of
father or mother, whether I speak, keep silence,
sit, stand, or go, eat, drink, be merry, or sad, be
sewing, playing, dancing, or doing any thing else,
I must do it as it were in such weight, measure,
and number, even so perfectly as God made the
world; or else I am so sharply taunted, so cruelly
threatened, yea, presently sometimes with pinches,
nips, and bobs, and other ways, which I will not
name for the honour I bear them; so without measure disordered, that I think myself in hell till the
time come that I must go to Mr. Elmer, who
teacheth me so gently, so pleasantly, with such fair
allurements to learning, that I think all the time
nothing, whilst 1 am with him; and when I am
called from him. I fall on weeping, because what-

soever I do else but learning is full of great trouble, fear, and whole misliking unto me; and thus
my book hath been so much my pleasure, and
bringeth daily to me more pleasure, and more that
in respect of it all other pleasures in very deed be
but trifles and troubles unto me." A long letter
from Ascham to Lady Jane after this interview,
which is the last he ever had with her, dated in
January 1551-2, is extant, containing the most en-
couraging expressions to prosecute her studies, but
mixed with the grossest, and when it is considered
that it was directed to a girl not quite fifteen years
old, the most injudicious flattery. If such was the
tone in which her tutors addressed her, she must
have been endowed with an extraordinary strength
of mind not to have become the most consummate
pedant; and from this and other specimens of the
homage paid her by several learned men, our
contempt for these literary sycophants is lost
in admiration of Lady Jane's character, that though
thus courted, she should have retained her native
diffidence and humility. It has been suggested
that the extraordinary, if not ridiculous, attention
paid her by the most eminent reformers with whom
she was contemporary, arose from an idea which
is supposed to have been prevalent that she was
destined to have been the consort of her cousin
Edward VI. If such was the cause of these

fulsome addresses the motive may lessen, but it cannot excuse a recourse to means so disgraceful to induce her to become the champion of their party.

The advocates of the reformation with justice claimed Lady Jane Grey as a proselyte to their faith: this attachment to the .protestant doctrines may be attributed to her tutors, and .to her intercourse with Queen Catharine Parr; and it became so deeply rooted in her heart, that as she afterwards evinced, no temptation, not even the promise of life and fortune, was sufficiently powerful to induce her to abandon them, and she has consequently been considered by the reformed writers as fully entitled to the crown of martyrdom. It must have been about this period that her first epistle in Latin to Henry Bullinger, one of the most distinguished of the protestant divines, which with a translation will be found in this volume, was written, and as each of these three celebrated letters are signed with her maiden name, it is certain that they were all composed before her marriage. How far they may be deemed Lady Jane's entire composition is at least problematical; she was then above fourteen, and had certainly studied the Latin language for many years, but on the other hand, it is very likely that her preceptor should have corrected, if he

did not wholly write them, and the conjecture
that they were sufficiently her own to justify their
being so considered, but that Aylmer prevented
any gross inaccuracy from appearing in them, is
probably not far from the real fact. On the 11th of
October, 1551, Edward VI. raised the Marquess
of Dorset to the Dukedom of Suffolk, a dignity
which became extinct on the death of the Marchioness' half-brother Henry Brandon, Duke of
of Suffolk, in that year, without issue; and on the
same day, John Dudley, Earl of Warwick, was
created Duke of Northumberland. Lady Jane
Grey had then just attained her fourteenth year,
and is considered to have first appeared in public
in her mother's train, on the occasion of the visit
of Mary, the Dowager Queen of Scotland to the
Court at Greenwich, and she shortly afterwards
became the guest of the Princess Mary. Fox
recites an anecdote that occured during her visit,
which conspicuously displays the quickness of her
wit. She was invited by Lady Anne Wharton,
who apparently was the daughter of George, Earl
of Shrewsbury, and second wife of Thomas, first
Lord Wharton, and was probably one of the attendants of the Princess, to accompany her in a
walk, and passing in their road the Princess' Chapel, Lady Anne made the customary obeisance of
a Catholic to a place of worship, from the Host

always being contained therein. Her companion not comprehending the object of her respect, asked if the Princess Mary were in the chapel, and was answered in the negative, with the explanation that she had made her curtesy to him that made us all, "how can he be there that made us all," ingeniously observed Lady Jane, "when the baker made him?" "This answer," Fox asserts, "coming to the Lady Mary's ears, she did never love her after, as is credibly reported, but esteemed her as the rest of that christian profession."[a] Somerset, who had resigned the Protectorship three years before, was at the instigation of the Duke of Northumberland, who deemed him an obstacle to his plans, arrested in October, 1552, and in December following, he was arraigned on the charges of high treason and felony; and after a trial which Hume describes as being attended with more formality than was usual at that period, he was acquitted of treason, but adjudged guilty of felony, for which crime his judges condemned him to death. Considerable care had been taken by Dudley, to prevent any merciful intentions arising in the breast of Edward to impede his uncle's execution, and to the lively grief of the people, this once powerful nobleman was beheaded on Tower-hill, on the 22nd January, 1553.

[a] *Acts and Monuments.*

The young monarch, naturally of a weak constitution, and who had in the preceding year been attacked both with the measles and small-pox, caught a severe cold at the commencement of the year 1553, which so seriously affected his health, that being unable to meet the Parliament, which assembled in March, at Westminster, they were obliged to attend his Majesty at Whitehall, and after sitting only a month it was dissolved. The health of the king now became the subject of considerable anxiety, as symptoms of a consumptive nature shewed themselves, and though much hope was placed in his youth and temperance, great fears were expressed as to the result of his illness. It was at this crisis that the germs of Northumberland's ambition budded with vigour and effect: and as he had not the slightest pretensions to the royal dignity himself, it became the object of his most anxious wishes to produce an alliance between his family and the blood royal. For this purpose Lady Jane Grey presented an unexceptionable opportunity; as the daughter of the Duke of Suffolk, the union with his son was an alliance equal in every respect to her expectations, hence he could scarcely anticipate an obstacle to the proposition; and to a mind disposed to bend every thing to its wishes, and possessed of sufficient power to effect what it desired, the following facts

e

afforded his intended daughter-in-law some pretensions to the throne. Henry VIII. had under
the authority of Parliament, by his will entailed
the crown, first on his son, Edward Prince of
Wales, and his issue; in default of which on his
daughter the Princess Mary and her children;
and if she died issueless, on his daughter the Princess Elizabeth and her descendants: in the event
of their decease without lawful issue, the royal dignity was, contrary to the general rules of succession, to descend to the children of his nieces, the
daughters of his younger sister, Mary, Queen
Dowager of France, then the wife of Charles Brandon, Duke of Suffolk; namely, Lady Frances,
afterwards Duchess of Suffolk, and Lady Eleanor,
who married the Earl of Cumberland. In this
settlement of the crown,[a] two peculiarities are to
be observed; first, that the descendants of his
Majesty's *eldest* sister Margaret, Queen of Scotland, were removed, to make way for the descendants of his *youngest* sister; and, what is still
more singular, under that settlement, his nieces
themselves never could have succeeded to the

[a] For a full account of the Statutes passed relative to
the succession during the reign of Henry VIII., under two
of which he derived the power to limit the descent of the
Crown by his Will, the reader is referred to a note at the
end of the memoir.

throne, but the eldest son, or the issue of the eldest
son ; or in default of issue male, the eldest daughter, or the child of the eldest daughter of Frances,
Duchess of Suffolk, would have inherited the
crown, even if the Duchess had been still living :
an anomaly so glaring, that it can only be
accounted for on the supposition, that when
Henry's will was framed, the possibility of his
nieces' surviving his children, who were all many
years younger than their cousins, was not contemplated.   This disposition of the royal dignity,
had been solemnly ratified by Parliament,[a] so that
on the demise of Edward VI., his half-sister
Mary, was the undoubted heiress to the throne,
according to the laws of descent, that regulated
the succession previous to the Testament of her
father, and likewise agreeable to the express provisions in that instrument; but as Henry's marriages with Katharine of Arragon and Ann Boleyn,
had both been declared null and void, the Princesses Mary and Elizabeth were thereby rendered
illegitimate.   Under these circumstances, and
actuated by motives which cannot be mistaken,
Dudley was anxious to secure the hand of Lady
Jane, for his fourth son, Lord Guildford Dud-

a 35 Hen. VIII. cap. i. and 1 Edw. VI. Cap. xii. see
the note at the end of the memoir.

ley, his three other sons being already married; and as no objections were urged by her parents, the union took place about the end of May, in 1553; for the state of the monarch's health was too precarious to admit of delay, and Northumberland's object would not have been secured, had he obtained the wished for alteration in the succession, before the future Queen had become the wife of his son. This important point gained, it only remained for the crafty statesman to avail himself of every means to influence Edward to make such a disposition of the Crown, as would complete his ambitious designs. As he was thoroughly aware of the young monarch's stedfast attachment to the reformed religion, and as Mary had unequivocally displayed her resolute adherence to the old faith, he possessed powerful arguments with which to persuade Edward to set aside his sister, by making a new settlement of the throne. Having thus the amiable monarch's religious fears to work upon, when he was in that state which induces men to think seriously of their eternal welfare, and when they are feverishly eager to grasp at every means which they are advised will tend to it, can it be a matter of surprize, that he should have yielded to Northumberland's representations and entreaties? We are informed that the King was

much pleased when acquainted with his cousin's
marriage, and in his dying hours he evidently
considered that she would be his successor.
After the monarch's consent had been gained, it
became necessary for Dudley to procure that of
the Council, and the ground on which the alteration in the succession was urged, was, that Mary
had been declared illegitimate by Act of Parliament;[a] but as it was not sufficient for his purpose
that she should be rendered incapable of inheriting
the crown, unless her half-sister Elizabeth was included in the disability, the dissolution of the
marriage of her mother,[b] by which she had in
effect also been bastardized, was urged with considerable plausibility, both to the Sovereign and
his Council.   Edward would probably gladly
have settled the royal dignity on the Princess
Elizabeth, whose attachment to the protestant religion was generally admitted, but the injustice
would have been too flagrant had the Act of Parliament which incapacitated Mary been revived,
whilst that which created a similar inability in
Elizabeth, remained unnoticed.   If Edward's earnest wishes for the security of the new religion
were to be realized, but one course was open, and
which was ultimately adopted, by his settling the

a 25 Hen. VIII. cap. xix.
b 28 Hen. VIII. cap. vii.

crown on a protestant. To effect this object,
however, considerable caution. was necessary;
and as it is an undisputed fact, that no arrange-
ment would have obtained Dudley's concurence,
which did not tend to vest the sceptre in the hand of
his daughter-in-law, the alteration from the course
prescribed by the will of Henry, was certainly as
slight and as apparently consonant to justice, as
was possible. Edward is said to have objected,
that if Mary and Elizabeth were set aside, the
Duchess of Suffolk would be the next heir, but
this statement must either be an unfounded conjecture, or made in ignorance of the facts of the
case, for in no way could she have been heir to
the crown. By the laws of descent, the next
-heir to the throne, after the disqualification of
the two Princesses, was the celebrated Mary,
Queen of Scots, mother of James I., she being the
daughter and heiress of James V., King of Scotland, son and heir of James IV. of Scotland, by
Margaret, the *eldest* sister of Henry VIII.;[a] and,
as has been already remarked, the will of that
monarch never created a right in the mother
of Lady Jane Grey, though the crown was limited to her daughters, a circumstance which is
totally unnoticed by Hume, and by most other
historians. Thus, if Mary and Elizabeth were

[a] Vide the accompanying Genealogical Table.

disqualified, Lady Jane Grey, was, according to
the provisions in her grand-uncle's will, the undoubted heiress to the throne, and considering the
violent change which was created in the succession by Edward, in prefering his cousin to his
half-sister, the grounds on which it was effected
were certainly extremely plausible, for it was sim-
ply to revive the statutes which had declared
Henry's first and second marriages void, and then
to act upon the other parts of the settlement under
that monarch's will, in the same manner as if death
had rendered the two Princesses as naturally, as
their being declared illegitimate would have made
them legally incapable of succeeding to the royal,
or to any other dignity. It is very far from the
object of these remarks, to defend the venality of
Henry's Parliaments, which so entirely rendered
themselves the instrument of their sovereign's
lust and caprice; a venality which has never been
so beautifully described by a native, as by a
foreign pen, and the justice of which will excuse
the introduction of the passage alluded to: it is
supposed to be the reply of Mary Queen of Scot's, to
the arguments of Burleigh, that no tribunal could
be more impartial, than that before which she was
about to be arraigned, as its members were se-
lected from the chief nobility of England.

"Yes, truly; were these Lords as you describe them,
I must be mute; my cause beyond all hope
Were lost, if such a Court pronounce me guilty.
But, Sir, these names, which you are pleased to praise,
These very men, whose weight you think will crush me,
I see performing in the history
Of these dominions, very different parts:
I see this high nobility of England,
This grave majestic Senate of the realm,
Like to an eastern monarch's vilest slaves,
Flatter my uncle Henry's sultan fancies:
I see this noble rev'rend House of Lords,
Venal alike with the corrupted Commons,
Make Statutes and annul them, ratify
A marriage, and dissolve it, as the voice
Of power commands: to-day it disinherits,
And brands the royal daughters of the realm
With the vile name of bastards, and to-morrow
Crowns them as Queen's, and leads them to the throne.
I see them in four reigns, with pliant conscience,
Four times abjure their faith; renounce the Pope
With Henry, yet retain the old belief;
Reform themselves with Edward; hear the Mass
Again with Mary; with Elizabeth,
Who governs now, reform themselves again.[a]"

Though Edward and the Council had acceded
to Northumberland's plans, it appears that both
menace and flattery were used to obtain the ap-
probation of the Judges. Sir Edward Montague,
the Chief Justice of the Common Pleas, together

---

[a] Schiller's *Mary Stuart.*

with Sir John Baker and Sir Thomas Bromley, two
of the other Judges, and the Attorney and Solicitor General, being summoned before the Council,
the proposed succession was explained to them;
when they were commanded by the King to
draw up the intended instrument, in the form of
Letters Patent. They hesitated to obey, desiring time to consider of it, and according to
Hume, the more they reflected, the greater danger
they found in compliance. They urged that the
settlement of the crown by Henry VIII. had not only
been confirmed by an Act of Parliament, but by another Act passed in the early part of Edward's reign
it was declared treason, in any one, to attempt to
change the order of the succession, and they
properly felt, that nothing but Parliament could
legally alter the limitations as then settled, and advised the king to summons that assembly without
delay: it was on the occasion of one of these
discussions, that Dudley's zeal overpowered his
discretion, as he is reported to have called Montague a traitor, and to have expressed his readiness to fight any man in his shirt, in so just a
cause as the succession of Lady Jane. After many
debates, Sir Edward Montague proposed an expedient, which the ingenuity of a lawyer only
could have devised. He suggested that a special
commission should be passed by the King and

f

Council, requiring the Judges to draw a Patent
for the new settlement of the Crown, and that a
pardon should immediately after be granted them
for any offence which they might have committed
by obeying the mandate. This expedient satisfied
the Council and his colleagues, but when the Patent was drawn, and brought to James Goodriche,
Bishop of Ely, the Chancellor, to receive the
great seal, he refused to affix it, unless the whole of
the Judges should previously sign it. All of them
acceded to the request without difficulty, excepting Sir John Hales, one of the Judges of the
Court of Common Pleas, and William Gosnold,
the Solicitor General; the latter intimitated by
the violent threats of Northumberland, at length
complied; but Hales, though a protestant, could
not be prevailed upon to do violence to his conscience, "preferring," adds Hume, "on this occasion, justice to the prejudices of his party."
The Chancellor's scruples were however not yet
satisfied, and he next required, that all the Privy
Councillors should likewise sign it; and the influence of Northumberland was so extensive, that
each of them thus testified his consent to the important document.

It may be expected that more should be said
on Lady Jane's marriage, but little beyond conjecture can be expressed as to how far her own

inclinations coincided with the choice of her parents ; but the presumption is in favour of affection
being as predominant in her union, as was usual in
marriages at that period, between parties of their
rank in life.   According to some authorities, Lady
Katharine Grey, her sister, was married on the
same day, to her first husband, William Lord Herbert, son and heir of Henry, first Earl of Pembroke,
but from whom she was afterwards divorced. These
nuptials we are told, were celebrated with great
splendour; from the time of her marriage, until
the death of Edward, it has been said[a] that she
resided with her husband's family at Sion House,
and as a proof of her studies not having been
neglected, it is stated that her third letter to Bullinger, was written from that mansion; but this
assertion is however erroneous, for it will be seen
in a subsequent page, not only that the letter in
question was signed with her maiden name, but she
expressly observes: "Magnaque præterea mihi
spes est te huic mea plusquam muliebri audatiæ,
quæ virgo ad virum, et indocta ad eruditionis patrem scribere audeam, ignoscere," from which
passage it is manifest that it was written before
her marriage.

Edward VI. died on the 6th of July, 1553,

---

[a] *Lady Jane Grey and her Times*, p. 220.

and it of course became necessary that the new succession should be instantly promulgated. Historians concur in stating, that until the monarch's decease, Lady Jane was not only totally uninformed of the important measures which her father-in-law had taken in her favour, but that she received the intimation of them, and of the greatness which awaited her, with the deepest sorrow. It matters but little in what manner the news was imparted to her, whether, as is stated by Hume, on the authority of Thuanus, Burnet, and Heylyn, by Northumberland and her own father, together with the Earl of Pembroke, and some of the other nobility, approaching her with the respect due to royalty; or privately by her mother; but it is of considerable value in estimating her character, that her conduct on the occasion should be fully examined. Her excellent judgment probably taught her the real dangers of her situation, and the humility of her heart prevented that judgment from being blinded by the dazzling offer of the imperial diadem. We are expressly told, that at first she resolutely refused the proffered dignity, urging with no less good sense than justice, the superior claims of her cousins, the Princesses Mary and Elizabeth; and in reply to their arguments, Heylyn states, " that Northumberland's speech being ended, the poor

lady found herself in a great perplexity, not knowing whether she should more lament the death of
the King, or her adoption to the kingdom: the
first loss not to be repaired; the next care possible to be avoided. She looked upon the crown as
a great temptation, to resist which, she stood in
need of all the helps, which both philosophy and
divinity could suggest unto her. And she knew
also that such fortunes seldom knocked twice for
entrance at the same man's gate; but that if once
refused they are gone for ever. Taking some-
time, therefore, for deliberation, she summoned a
council of her purest thoughts; by whose advice,
half drowned in tears (either as sorrowing for the
King's death, or foreseeing her own), she returned
an answer in these words, or to this effect:—
'That the laws of the kingdom, and natural right
standing for the King's sister, she would beware
of burthening her weak conscience with a yoke
which did belong to them; that she understood
the infamy of those who had permitted the viola-
tion of right to gain a sceptre; that it were to mock
God, and deride justice, to scruple at the stealing
of a shilling, and not at the usurpation of a crown.
—'Besides,' said she, 'I am not so young, nor
so little read in the guiles of fortune, as to
suffer myself to be taken by them. If she enrich
any, it is but to make them the subject of her

spoil; if she raise others, it is but to pleasure herself with their ruins. What she adored but yesterday, to day is her pastime. And if I now permit her to adorn and crown me, I must tomorrow suffer her to crush and tear me to pieces. Nay, with what crown doth she present me? A crown which hath been violently and shamefully wrested from Catharine of Arragon; made more unfortunate by the punishment of Ann Bulloign, and others that wore it after her. And why then would you have me add my blood to theirs; and be the third victim from whom this fatal crown may be ravished with the head that wears it? But in case it should not prove fatal unto me, and that all its venom were consumed; if fortune should give me warranties of her constancy; should I be well advised to take upon me these thorns which would dilacerate, though not kill me outright; to burthen myself with a yoke which would not fail to torment me, though I were assured not to be strangled with it? My liberty is better than the chain you proffer me, with what precious stones soever it be adorned, or of what gold soever framed. I will not exchange my peace for honourable and precious jealousies, for magnificent and glorious fetters. And if you love me sincerely, and in good earnest, you will rather wish me a secure and quiet fortune, though mean, than an exalted condition exposed to the wind, and followed by some dismal fall.'"

Happy would it have been had she persevered in so wise a determination, but the vehement solicitations of her father, and especially of Northumberland, her father-in-law, ultimately overcame her reluctance, and a resolution which the suggestions of ambition could not seduce, gave way to the entreaties and commands, rather than to the arguments of her parents. A husband's has been said to have been added to parental authority on the occasion, and as Mr. Howard has well remarked, "Lord Guildford Dudley, dazzled by so brilliant a destiny, was prevailed on to add the accents of love, to the wiles of ambition, and beyond this female fortitude could not be expected to go." A motive to her acquiescence more powerful than any that have been hitherto attributed to her, is to be found in her reflection on the imminent danger in which those nearest to her heart were placed, and which nothing but her possession of the royal dignity could avert. The failure of a treasonable plot never fails to produce the destruction of those who created it, and she might reasonably have expected that the hour which saw Mary secure on the throne, would have been the last of the existence of her father, and the father of her husband. This dreadful truth must

have flashed on Lady Jane's mind, and she naturally
adopted the only step which could possibly secure
their safety. If this feeling operated on her judgment, and every circumstance tends to persuade us
that it did, her character appears in a new and
more lovely light, than it has before been exhibited; we see her thus consenting to incur the
utmost personal peril, by adopting a course contrary to the dictates of her conscience, with the
desperate hope of preserving her family. Her
consent thus extorted from her, she was the next
day conveyed by her father-in-law with great state
to the Tower, which fortress, according to long
established etiquette, had been the residence of
the Sovereigns for the first few day after their
accession; and she was immediately afterwards
proclaimed Queen of England, with the usual for-
malities, and in the following words:

"Jane, by the grace of God, Queen of England, France, and Ireland, Defender of the Faith
and of the Church of England, and also of Ireland,
under Christ on earth the supreme head. To all
our loving, faithful, and obedients, and to every
of them, greeting. Whereas our most dear cousin
Edward the Sixth, late King of England, France,
and Ireland, Defender of the Faith, and on earth
the supreme head under Christ of the Church of
England and Ireland, by his letters patent, signed

with his own hand, and sealed with his great seal
of England, bearing date the 21st day of June, in
the vith year of his reign, in the presence of the
most part of his nobles, his counsellors, judges, and
divers other grave and sage personages, for the
profit and surety of the whole realm thereto assenting, and subscribing their names to the same,
both by the same his letters patents recited that,
forasmuch as the imperial crown of this realm,
by an act made in the thirty-fifth year of the reign
of the late king of worthy memory, King Henry
the VIII. our progenitor and great uncle, for lack
of issue of his body lawfully begot, and for lack
of issue of the body of our said late cousin King
Edward the VI. by the same act limited and appointed to remain to the Lady Mary, by the name
of the Lady Mary, his eldest daughter, and to the
heirs of her body lawfully begot, and for the default of such issue the remainder thereof to the
Lady Elizabeth, by the name of the Lady Elizabeth, his second daughter, and to the heirs of her
body lawfully begotten, with such conditions as
should be limited and appointed by the said late
king of worthy memory, King Henry the Eight,
our progenitor and great uncle, by his letters patents under the great seal, or by his last will in
writing, signed with his hand. And, forasmuch
as the said limitation of the imperial crown of

this realm, being limited as is aforesaid to the said
Lady Mary and Lady Elizabeth being illegitimate,
and not lawfully begotten, for that the marriage
had between the said late king, King Henry the
VIII., our progenitor and great uncle, and the
Lady Katherine, mother to the said Lady Mary;
and also the marriage had between the said late
king, King Henry VIII., our progenitor and great
uncle, and the Lady Anna, mother to the said
Lady Elizabeth, were clearly and lawfully undone
by sentences of divorces, according to the word
of God, and the ecclesiastical laws, and which
said several divorcements have been severally ratified and confirmed by authority of parliament,
and especially in the twenty-eighth year of the
reign of King Henry VIII., our progenitor and
great uncle, remaining in force, strength, and
effect, whereby as well the said Lady Mary, as
also the said Lady Elizabeth, to all intents and
purposes, are, and been thereby disabled to ask,
claim, or challenge the said imperial crown, or
any other of the honours, castles, manors, lordships, lands, tenements, or other hereditaments,
as heir or heiress to our said late cousin, King
Edward the VI., or as heir or heiress to any
other person or persons whosoever, as well for
the cause before rehearsed, as also for that the
said Lady Mary and Elizabeth were unto our said

late cousin but of the half blood, and therefore by
the ancient laws, statutes, and customs of this
realm be not inheritable unto our said late cousin,
although they had been born in lawful matrimony,[a]
as indeed they were not, as by the said sentences
of divorce, and the said statute of the twenty-eighth
year of the reign of our King Henry VIII., our
said progenitor and great uncle, plainly appeareth;
and forasmuch also as it is to be thought, or at
the least much to be doubted, that if the said Lady
Mary or Lady Elizabeth should hereafter have and
enjoy the said imperial crown of this realm, and
should happen to marry with any stranger born
out of this realm, that the said stranger having
the government and the imperial crown in his
hands would adhere and practise, not only to
bring this noble free realm into the tyranny and

[a] The fallacy of this assertion, though sufficiently ob-
vious at the present day, was not entirely destitute of force
at the period in question; for perhaps it was not then so
settled a point of law, that the rule of *possessio fratris*, does
not apply to the Crown, or to any other dignity: Blackstone, *Commentaries*, Book I. Chap. iii. p. 193, in proof of
the fact in relation to the descent of the Crown, cites Mary's
having succeeded Edward VI. but as there was no such
precedent when that succession was in dispute, it is not
extraordinary that to suit the case in point, an attempt
should have been made to,assimilate the descent of the royal
dignity with that of common inheritances.

servitude of the Bishop of Rome, but also to have
the laws and customs of his, or their own native
country or countries, to be practised, and put in
use within this realm, rather than the laws, statutes, and customs here of long time used, whereupon the title of inheritance of all, and singular
the subjects of this realm do depend, to the peril
of conscience, and the utter subversion, of the
common weal of this realm. Whereupon our said
late dear cousin, weighing and considering with
himself what ways and means were most convenient to be had for the stay of the said succession
in the said imperial crown, if it should please God
to call our said late cousin out of this transitory
life, having no issue of his body, and calling to his
rememberance that we and the Lady Katherine
and the Lady Mary, our sisters, being the daughters of the Lady Frances, our natural mother, and
then and yet wife to our natural and most loving
father, Henry, Duke of Suffolk, and the Lady
Margaret, daughter of the Lady Eleanor then deceased sister to the said Lady Frances, and the
late wife of our cousin Henry, Earl of Cumberland, were very nigh of his grace's blood, of the
part of his father's side, our said progenitor and
great uncle, and being naturally born here within
the realm, and for the very good opinion our said
late cousin had of our, and our said sisters and

cousin Margaret's good education, did therefore
upon good deliberation and advice herein had, and
taken, by his said letters patents declare, order,
assign, limit, and appoint, that if it should fisr
tune himself, our said late cousin King Edward
the Sixth to decease, having no issue of his body
lawfully, begotten, that then the said imperial
crown of England and Ireland, and the confines of
the same, and his title to the crown of the realm
of France, and all and singular honours, castles,
prerogatives, privileges, preliminaries, authorities,
jurisdictions, dominions, possessions, and hereditaments, to our said late cousin, King Edward the
Sixth, or to the said imperial crown belonging, or
in anywise appertaining, should, for lack of such
issue of his body, remain, come, and be unto the
eldest son of the body of the said Lady Frances
lawfully begotten, and so from son to son, as he
should be of ancienty in birth, of the body of the
said Lady Frances lawfully begotten, being born
into the world in our said cousin's life-time, and
to the heirs-male of the body of every such son
lawfully begotten; and for default of such son
born into the world in his life-time, of the body of
the said Lady Frances, lawfully begotten, and for
lack of heirs-male of every such son lawfully begotten, that then the said imperial crown, and all
and singular other the premises should remain,

come, and be to us, by the name of the Lady
Jane, eldest daughter of the said Lady Frances,
and to the heirs-male of our body lawfully begotten, that then the said imperial crown, and all
other the premises, should remain, come, and be
to the said Lady Katharine, our said second sister,
and to the heirs-male of the body of the said Lady
Katherine lawfully begotten, with divers other
remainders, as by the same letters patents more
plainly at large it may and doth appear. Sithens
the making of which letters patents, that is to say,
on Thursday, which was the sixth day of this instant, month of July, it hath pleased God to call
to his infinite mercy our said most dear and entirely beloved cousin Edward the Sixth, whose soul
God pardon, and forasmuch as he is now deceased
having no heirs of his body begotten, and that also
there remaineth at this present time no heirs lawfully begotten of the body of our said progenitor
and great uncle, King Henry VIII. and forasmuch
also as the said Lady Frances, our said mother,
had no issue male begotten of her body, and born
into the world in the life-time of our said cousin,
King Edward the Sixth, so as the said imperial
crown, and other the premises to the same belonging, or in anywise appertaining, now be, and
remain to us in actual and royal possession, by
authority of the said letters patents : We do there-

fore, by these presents, signify unto all our most
loving, faithful, and obedient subjects, that like as
we for our part shall, by God's grace, shew ourselves a most gracious and benign sovereign
Queen, and Lady to all our good subjects, in all
their just and lawful suits and- causes, and to the
uttermost of our power shall preserve and maintain God's most holy word, Christian Polity, and
the good Lawes, Customs, and Liberties of these
our realms and dominions; so we mistrust not,
but they and every of them, will again, for their
parts, at all times and in all cases, shew themselves unto us their natural liege Queen and Lady,
most faithful, loving, and obedient subjects, according to their bounden duties and allegiances,
whereby they shall please God, and do the thing
that shall tend to their own preservations and
sureties: willing and commanding all men of all
estates, degrees, and conditions to see our peace
and accord kept, and to be obedient to our laws,
as they tender our favour, and will answer for the
contrary at their extreme perils. In witness
whereof we have caused these our letters to be
made patents. Witness, ourself at our Tower of
London, this tenth day of Julie, in the first year
of our reign.

"God save the Queen."[a]

[a] Lansdowne MSS. 198, f. 9-14, into which it is transcribed from the copy printed by Grafton, in 1553. There

It was the commands of the Council, that she should also be proclaimed throughout the kingdom, but those orders were executed only in London and its neighbourhood, and we are told that it was heard in silence, and with regret. Nor was the eloquence of the pulpit, which was zealously exerted in favour of her title; attended with success, as a proof of which, the sermon of Ridley, Bishop of London, who preached to the same purpose, produced no effect on his audience.

In the mean time, Mary was neither an unconcerned nor an idle spectator of this serious attempt to deprive her of her birthright. She wrote[a] to the Council on the 9th of July, claiming the Crown as her inheritance, and expressed her surprize that the demise of her brother had not been duly notified to her. The answer of the Council to this application, is too curious a document not to be given at length.

" Madam,

" We have received your letters, the ix of this instant, declaring your supposed title, which you judge yourself to have to the Imperial Crown of this realm, and all the dominions thereunto belonging. For answer whereof, this is to adver-

is also an imperfect copy of part of this Proclamation in Cottonian MSS., Julius F. vi. f. 194.

[a] Printed in Fox's *Acts and Monuments*, folio, p. 1567.

tise you, that for as much as our Sovereign Lady
Queen Jane, is, after the death of our Sovereign
Lord Edward VI., a prince of most noble memory,
invested and possessed with the just and right
title in the Imperial Crown of this realm, not only
by good order of old ancient good laws of this
realm, but also by our late Sovereign Lord's Letters Patent, signed with his own hand, and sealed
with the great seal of England, in presence of the
most part of the nobles, counsellors, judges, with
divers other grave and sage personages assenting
and subscribing to the same. We must therefore,
as of most bound duty and allegiance, assent unto
her said Grace, and to none other; except we
should, which faithful subjects cannot, fall into
grievous and unspeakable enormities, wherefore
we can no less do, but for the quiet both of the
realm and you, also to advertise you, that forasmuch as the divorce made between the King of
famous memory, K. Henry VIII., and the Lady
Katharine your mother, was necessary to be had
both by the everlasting laws of God, and also by
ecclesiastical laws, and also by the most part of
the noble and learned universities of Christendom,
and confirmed also by the sundry acts of Parliament remaining yet in their force, and thereby you
justly made illegitimate and uninheritable to the
Crown Imperial of this realm, and the rules, domi-

h

nions, and possessions of the same, you will upon just consideration hereof, and of divers other causes, lawful to be alleged for the same, and for the just inheritance of the right line and godly orders, taken by the late King, our Sovereign Lord King Edward VI., and agreed upon by the nobles and greatest personages aforesaid, surcease by any pretence to vex and molest any of our Sovereign Lady Queen Jane, her subjects, from their true faith and allegiance due unto her Grace: assuring you, that if you will for respect show yourself quiet and obedient, as you ought, you shall find us all and several ready to do you any service that we with duty may, and be glad with your quietness to preserve the common state of this realm, wherein you may be otherwise grievous unto us, to yourself, and to them. And thus we bid you most heartily well to fare. From the Tower of London, this ix of July, 1553.

"Your Ladyship's friends, shewing yourself an obedient subject.

"THOMAS CANTERBURY,
THE MARQUESS OF WINCHESTER,
JOHN BEDFORD,
W. NORTHAMPTON,
THOMAS ELY, CHANCELLOR,
NORTHUMBERLAND,
HENRY SUFFOLK,
HENRY ARUNDEL,
SHREWSBURY,
PEMBROKE,
COBHAM,
R. RITCH,
HUNTINGDON,
DARCY,
CHEYNY,
R. COTTON,
JOHN GATES,
W. PETER,
W. CICELLE,
JOHN CHEKE,
JOHN MASON,
EDW. NORTH,
R. BOWES."

Mary had removed from Hovesdon to her manor of Keninghall, in Norfolk; and as she had lately lost one of her household servants by the plague, the pretence for her journey was the fear of infection; but from Keninghall she very soon went to her castle of Framlingham, in Suffolk, where she assumed the royal title. The inhabitants of Suffolk tendered her their homage, as their legitimate sovereign, though they mingled their declarations of alarm for the reformed religion, with the assurances of loyalty; but when she pledged herself that she never meant to change the laws of the late monarch,* they enlisted themselves in her cause with considerable ardour. Many of the chief nobility and gentry daily flocked to her standard, and in a very short time she found herself in a situation to enforce by arms the pretensions which her birth and the laws of the Realm so unequivocally afforded her.

The three letters written in Lady Jane Grey's name, during her usurpation of the royal dignity, announcing her succession to the throne, and

* Fox relates, that when they afterwards prayed her to fulfil this promise, she replied : " for so much as you being but members, desire to rule your head, you shall one day well perceive that members must obey their head, and not look to bear rule over the same," *Acts and Monuments*, 1570, folio, p. 1568.

ordering certain measures to be taken to secure
her in the possession of it, are too important to
be omitted in this memoir.

"JANE, THE QUEEN,

"Right trusty and right well beloved Cousin, we greet you well, advertising the same,
that whereas it hath pleased Almighty God to call
to his mercy out of this life our dearest cousin the
King your late Sovereign Lord, by reason
whereof and such ordinances as the said late
King did establish in his life time for the security and wealth of this Realm, we are entered
into our rightful possession of this Kingdom, as
by the last Will of our said dearest Cousin, our
late progenitor, and other several instruments to
that effect, signed with his own hand and sealed
with the great Seal of this Realm in his own
presence, whereunto the nobles of this realm for
the most part and all our Council and Judges,
with the Mayor and Aldermen of our City of
London, and divers other grave personages of this
our Realm of England have also subscribed their
names as by the same will and instrument it may
more evidently and plainly appear : We therefore do
You to understand, that by the ordinance and suf-
ferance of the heavenly Lord and King, and by
the assent and consent of our said Nobles and

Counsellors, and others before specified, we do this day make our entry into our Tower of London, as rightful Queen of this Realm; and have accordingly set forth our proclamations to all our loving subjects giving them thereby to understand their duties and allegiance which they now of right owe unto us as more amply by the same you shall briefly perceive and understand; nothing doubting, right trusty and right well beloved Cousin, but that you will endeavour yourself in all things to the uttermost of your power, not only to defend our just title, but also assist us in our rightful possession of this Kingdom, and to disturb, repel, and resist the feigned and untrue claim of the Lady Mary, bastard daughter to our great uncle, Henry the Eight of famous memory: wherein as you shall do that which, to your honour, truth, and duty appertaineth, so shall we remember the same unto you and yours accordingly.   And our further pleasure is that you shall continue, do, and execute every thing and things as our Lieutenant within all places, according to the tenor of the Commission addressed unto you from our late Cousin, King Edward the vjth, in such and like sort as if the same had been, as we mind shortly it shall be, renewed, and by us confirmed under our Great Seal unto you.

" Given under our signet at our Tower of London the xjth of July the first year of our Reign.

" To our right trusty and right well beloved Cousin and Counsellor the Marquis of Northampton, our Lieutenant General of our County of Surrey, and to our trusty and well beloved the Deputies of that Lieutenancy, and the Sheriff, the chief Justices of Peace, and the worshipful of that Shire."[a]

By the Queen.

" JANE, the Queen,

" Trusty and well beloved we greet you well. Albeit that our estate in this imperial Crown whereof we be actually and really possessed, as partly may appear by our Proclamation, wherein our title is published, is not, nor can be in any wise doubtful to all such our good faithful subjects, as setting blind affection apart, do with reason and wisdom consider the very foundation and ground of our title, with the great commodities thereby coming through God's providence to the preservation of our common weal and poli-

[a] Ellis' *Original Letters Illustrative of English History*, vol. ii. p. 183, from the original among the Muniments at Loseley House.

cy; yet for that we understand the Lady Mary
doth not cease by Letters in her name, provoked
thereto by her adherents, enemies of this Realm,
to publish and notify slanderously to divers of
of our subjects matter derogatory to our title and
dignity royal, with the slander of certain of our
Nobility and Council : We have thought meet to
admonish and exhort You, as our true and faithful
subjects, to remain fast in your obeisance and
duty to the Imperial Crown of this Realm,
whereof we have justly the possession; and not
to be removed any wise from your duty by
slanderous reports or letters, dispersed abroad
either by the said Lady Mary, or by her adherents; for truly like as the Nobility of our
Realm, our Council, our Prelates, our Judges, and
learned men, and others good wise men, godly
and natural subjects, do remain fast and surely in
their Allegiance towards us, ready to adventure
their lives, lands, and goods for our defence, so
can a great number of the same Nobility, Counsellors, and Judges, truly testify to all the
world, with safety of their conscience, how
carefully and earnestly the late King of famous
memory, our dear Cousin King Edward the
Sixth, from time to time mentioned and provoked
them partly by persuasion, partly command-
ments, to have such respect to his succession, if

God should call him to his mercy without issue,
as might be the preservation of the Crown in
the whole undefiled English blood ; and therefore
of his own mere motion, both by grant of his
Letters Patents, and by declaration of his will,
established the succession as it is declared by our
Proclamation. And for the testimony hereof to
the satisfaction of such as shall conceive any
doubt herein, We understand that certain of our
Nobility have written at this present, in some
part to admonish you of your duties, and to testify their knowledge of the truth of our title
and right. Wherefore we leave to proceed further
therein, being assured in the goodness of God,
that your hearts shall be confirmed to owe your
duty to us your sovereign Lady, who mean to
preserve this Crown of England in the royal
blood, and out of the   * of strangers and
papists, with the defence of all you our good subjects, your lives, lands, and goods, in our peace
against the invasions and violence of all foreign
or inward enemies and rebels. Given under our
Signet at our Tower of London, the xvj day of
July, in the first year of our reign.

"To our trusty and well beloved
the Sheriff, Justices of Peace, and

* This space is left in the original.

other Gentlemen of our County of Surrey, and to every of them."[a]

"JANE, THE QUEEN.[b]

"Trusty and well beloved we greet you well,
because we doubt not but this our most lawful
possession of the crown with the free consent of
the nobility of our realm, and other the states of
the same as both plainly known and accepted
of you, as our most loving subjects, therefore we
do not reiterate the same, but now most earnestly
will and require, and by authority hereof warrant
you to assemble, muster, and levy all the power
that you can possible make, either of your servants,
tenants, officers, or friends, as well horsemen as
footmen, repairing to our right trusty and right well
beloved cousins, the Earls of Arundel and Pembroke,[c] their tenants, servants, and officers, and
with the same to repair with all possible speed

[a] Ibid. p. 186. From the original among the Muniments at Loseley House. Mr. Ellis informs us, that this
letter was sealed with the signet of King Edward VI.,—the
arms of France and England quarterly, crowned; with the
letters E. R. at the sides.

[b] It is from this signature that the fac-simile under the
Portrait prefixed to this memoir has been taken.

[c] In the margin of the manuscript whence this letter
has been copied, but in a more modern hand, is this note—
"Tho' these earls at the time were plotting against her."

i

towards Buckinghamshire, for the repression and
subduing of certain tumults and rebellions moved
there against us and our crown by certain seditious men. For the repression whereof we have
given orders to divers others our good subjects,
and gentlemen of such degree as you are, to repair in like manner to the same parties. So as
we nothing doubt but upon the access of such
our loving subjects as be appointed for that purpose to the place where this seditious people yet
remain, the same shall either lack heart to abide
in their malicious purpose or else receive such
punishment and execution as they deserve, seeking
the destruction of their native country and the
subversion of all men in their degrees, by rebellion of the base multitude, whose rage being stirred,
as of late years hath been seen, must needs be the
confusion of the whole common weal. Wherefore our
special trust is in your courage, wisdom, and fide-
lities in this matter, to advance yourselves both with
power and speed to this enterprise, in such sort as
by the nobility and council shall be also prescribed
unto you. And for the sustentation of your charge
in this behalf, our said council, by our said com-
mandment, do further give order to your satisfaction, as by their letters also shall appear unto you.
And beside that, we do assure you of our special
consideration of this your service to us and our

crown, as expressly to the preservation of this our
realm and commonwealth.   Given under our
signet at the Tower of London, the xviiith day of
July, the first year of our reign."

"To our trusty and well beloved
Sir John Bridges and Sir Nicolas Poyntz,
Knights."[a]

The support of the Emperor Charles V. was
anxiously courted by the partizans of Lady Jane,
and the correspondence between the Council and
Sir Philip Hoby and Sir Richard Morrison, the
Commissioners from the late King to that monarch, develops so many curious facts that a particular notice of it cannot be deemed uninteresting.
Some of these letters are printed in *Lady Jane
Grey and her Times,* but a selection taken from
one of the Harleian Manuscripts[b] will be sufficient
for the purpose of this memoir.   The notification
of Edward's demise was dated on the 8th of July;
in which it is remarkable that no notice whatever
is taken of his successor, and the Commissioners
are merely directed to acquaint the Emperor
with the event, and to add that it was the conviction of the Council, that his Majesty would be
willing to preserve the amity which then existed
between the two countries.   The following was
the Commissioners' reply, from which it is mani-

[a] Harl. MSS. 416, f. 30.
[b] No. 523.

fest that extreme caution was used by the Emperor, as to giving any opinion on the important subject which then agitated this country.

"TO THE LORDS OF THE COUNCIL,

"Please it your good Lordships, the xvi of this month, we declared to the Emperor our heavy and sorrowful news, setting forth, after that your Lordship's assured good wills and readiness at all times to observe and maintain the ancient amity which had been always betwixt the realm of England and House of Burgundy, and other the Emperor's dominions, according to your Lordship's pleasures, signified to us in your letters of the ix day of this present month; for answer whereunto the Emperor said that he was right sorry for his part of these heavy news, whereby he perceived the loss of such a brother, and so good a friend both to him and to his countries, and considering that he was of such a great towardness, and of such a hope to do good, and be a stay in Christendom, his loss was so much the greater; and used in this behalf many good words to our late Sovereign Lord's commendation and declarations of his grief for his death: and touching, saith he, the amity which hath been betwixt me and my late good brother, our countries and subjects, as I have always had good will to the observance of the same, according to such treaties as were be-

twixt us, so now understanding by you, my Lords
of the Council's good inclinations, and minds to entertain and observe this amity for correspondency,
I both now have and shall have like good will to
keep and continue the same, and I thank them
for making me understand their good will herein;
with compliments of many other words to this
purpose. So that as far as we can perceive by his
words, he mindeth assuredly to keep amity with
us, yet to decipher him better herein, it were not
amiss in our opinions, when as your Lordship's
shall advertise him, either with some new league
or to tempt him what he will say to the old, or
by some other means, which your wisdoms can
better devise, &c. Dated the xvii July, 1553.*"

* Immediately following the transcript of this letter
in Harl. MSS. 523, f. 12, 13, this note occurs : " The King
hath written to the regent, signifying unto her, Mr.
Chamberlains recommendation, and also requiring her in all
his Majesty's affairs to give unto you Mr. H. Hobby, benign
audience and full credit." On which Mr. Howard, p. 231,
perhaps on the authority of the Harleian Catalogue, vol. i.
p. 334, lays considerable stress, as evidence that Lord
Guildford Dudley, "in right of his marriage, actually
assumed the title of King," but it is most probable that the
King there mentioned, was Edward VI., for there is no proof
whatever when the letter alluded to was written; and as
the copies of the state papers contained in that MS.

A letter written two days previously, from the Commissioners, merits considerable attention, as it affords us evidence that the Emperor's objection to Lady Jane's succession were not in the first instance considered as certain, and that the title of King was attributed to Lord Guildford Dudley by foreigners; a circumstance of less importance, but still of sufficient interest to render it worthy of a remark, is also afforded by this letter, that Don Diego was one of Lord Guildford's sponsors.

either were arranged without the least attention to order, or became so from the negligence of the binder, no conclusion can be drawn from the place where it occurs in the volume; in evidence of which, the letter which immediately follows the one in the text was dated in 1552, that which is the next in point of time is inserted in a mutilated state, in f. 1, whilst the despatch announcing the appointment of the Bishop of Norwich, as Mary's Ambassador to the Emperor, dated 1st August, 1553, is placed at f. 45, and the intermediate pages are occupied not only with the letters just cited, but with others of various dates between 1549 and 1552. Moreover it must be observed, that in the copies of these despatches, in the Cottonian MS. Galba B. xii. the note in question is not to be found. These remarks are only meant to extend to the inference to be deduced from the above-mentioned note, for it will hereafter be seen, that the title of "Majesty" was actually attributed to Lord Guildford Dudley abroad, though there is no circumstance on record to establish that he was so styled in this country.

TO THE COUNCIL.

" Please it your good Lordship's,

"'The xiiij of this present, Don Diego
found me, Sir Philip Hoby, and me Sir Richard
Morrison, walking in our Host's garden, and at
his first coming to us, entered into a long talk,
how much he was bound to owe his good will and
service to England, and therefore he could not
but at one time both sorrow with us for the loss
of our old master, a Prince of such virtue and
towardness, and also rejoice with us, that our
master which is departed, did ere he went, provide us of a King, in whom we had so many
causes to rejoice in, he made his excuses that he
had not* come to us the day before, laying the
stay thereof in D. Arras; for saith he, when I
told him I would come to you, and shew me a
partaker both of your sorrows and gladness, with
mind to make offer to the King's Majesty by you
both, of as much service as should lye in me, and
of as much as my friends and kinsmen were able
to do, in case D. Arras did think such my offer
could not offend the Emperor my master, D. Arras' advice was, that I should for a season defer
my going unto you, which as I did somewhat
against my will, so I am now very glad that I so

---

* This word is erased in the MS. but the sense of the
paragraph requires its retention.

did, for he telleth me now I may come to you,
and sorrow with you, and make all the offers that
I can to the King's Majesty, for I shall not only
not offend him in so doing, but I shall much please
his Majesty therewith; and therefore saith he, as
I am sorry that ye have lost so good a King, so
do I much rejoice that ye have so noble and so
toward a Prince to succeed him, and I promise
you, by the word of a gentleman, I will at all
times serve his Highness myself, and as many as
I shall be able to bring with me, if the Emperor
did call me to serve him. We said, we hitherto
had received the sorrowful news, but the glad
tidings were as yet come unto us by no letters;
we were glad to hear thus much, and wished that
we were able to tell him all, how things went at
home: saith he, I can tell you thus much.—The
King's Majesty for discharge of his conscience,
wrote a good piece of his Testament with his own
hand, barring both his sisters of the Crown, and
leaving it to the Lady Jane, niece to the French
Queen. Whether the two daughters be base or no,
or why it is done, we that be strangers have nothing to do with the matter; you are bound to
serve and obey his Majesty, and therefore it is
reason we take him for your King, whom the consent of the nobles of your country have allowed
for your King. I, saith he, for my part of all

others, am bound to be glad that his Majesty is
settled in this office; I was his god-father, and
will as willingly spend my blood in his service, as
any subject that he hath, as long as I shall see
the Emperor my master so willing to embrace
his Majesty's amity. Don Francisco de Este,
general of all the footmen Italians, is gone to his
charge in Milan, who at his departure made the
like offer, as long as his master and ours should
be friends, which he trusted should be ever, praying us at our return to utter it to the King's Majesty, and thus we humbly take our leaves of your
honors, from the Commissioners at Brussels, the
xv of July, 1553."

The following passage occurs in the MS. immediately after the preceding letter, but whether
it belonged to it or not, can only be conjectured.ᵃ

"That it hath liked your Grace to promise
to consider my suit, I most humbly thank you for
hoping your goodness will at convenient leisure
take a time to remember the same, and despatch
me."

The letter from the new Queen to the Commissioners, dated at the Tower, 12th July, 1553,
announcing her succession, was conveyed by Mr.
Shelley; and in the same Manuscript from which
the other letters were taken, is the copy of

ᵃ Vide the note to p. lxi.

a very important dispatch, from the Commissioners to the Council, announcing that the Emperor had ordered them to attend him without
delay, and that whilst they were preparing to obey.
the summons, Mr. Shelley had arrived; but before
they could possibly open his dispatches, a second
messenger reached them, commanding them instantly to attend his Majesty, so that the audience
of which it was the object of that dispatch to
give the particulars, occurred before they were
officially informed of Lady Jane's having assumed.
the royal dignity.   In that interview the Emperor
gave them plainly to understand, first, that he was
far from pleased that Edward had declared his
sister to be illegitimate, and limited the succession
in a different manner than his father had done:
secondly, he complained that his Ambassadors in
England could not obtain an audience since the
death of the late King: thirdly, he observed, that
the Dauphin might have pretensions to the English Crown in right of his wife, the Queen of
Scotland, who was the descendant of the eldest,
whilst Lady Jane was the representative of the
youngest sister: fourthly, he wished the differ-
ences between Lady Jane and Lady Mary should
be determined by Parliament, without force or
violence, and that Lady Mary should be married
to some nobleman of England, so that the realm

might remain in the same state, both in Policy
and Religion; fifthly, he expressed his dislike at
Mr. Dudley's being sent into France; and, lastly,
he declined giving an audience to Mr. Shelley, until
he knew from whom he came. To this communication Hoby and Morrison merely replied, that
they had had no regular intimation of the proceedings in England, but that Mr. Shelley had
just reached Brussels with important letters,
which they had not had time to examine; and
they promised to acquaint his Majesty the next day
with their contents: but Charles being well informed of the state of affairs in England, an'excuse was made to receiving them; and it was
clearly intimated, that no one could be admitted
from England in any other character than as
Mary's accredited agent.[a]

[a] The Emperor's dislike to the innovation in the order
of the succession may not only be rationally accounted for
on political grounds, but the near consanguinity between
Mary and himself, as is shewn below, was a sufficient motive
to render him hostile to every attempt against her interests.
Mary married in the following year Philip, King of Spain,
the Emperor's son.

Ferdinand, King of Spain, ob. 1516.

Johanna=Philip Arthur, Prince=Katherine=Henry VIII.
  ofAus- of Wales, ob.   King of
  tria.   1502.   .   England.
                            Mary, Queen of
The Emperor Charles V.   England, ob. 1558.
     ob. 1558.

The rapid success which attended Mary's
efforts to dispossess her rival of the power which
she had usurped, rendered Lady Jane's affairs
extremely critical; and even the veil of ambition,
which had hitherto blinded Northumberland, was
at last removed by a conviction of his dangerous
situation. He had levied forces which were assembled in London, but suspicion of his colleagues
had with much justice taken possession of his
mind, and dreading the effect of his absence from
the metropolis, he resolved to remain near the person of Lady Jane, and persuaded the Duke of Suffolk to take the command of the army: the filial tenderness of the young Queen, however, worked upon
by those who wished to remove him, magnified the
danger to which her father would be exposed, and
her remonstrance, added to the Duke's acquaintance with Suffolk's want of capacity, induced him
to undertake the direction of the troops in person.
Previous to his departure, he represented to the
Council that he was fully sensible of the double
danger which he incurred in this enterprise, both
with respect to Mary and to themselves; for if they
in his absence should waver in their present sentiments, they might secure their own safety by his
destruction, and "make themselves seem innocent in his guiltiness." To these shrewd observations one of the Lords replied, "your Grace

makes a doubt of that which cannot be, for which
of us all can wash his hands clean of this business?
and therefore it behoves us to be as resolute as
yourself." The Earl of Arundel, his brother-in-
law, to testify his resolution, remarked : "he was
sorry it was not his chance to go with him, at
whose feet he could find in his heart to spend his
best blood." On the 14th of July, Northumberland, accompanied by the Marquess of Northampton, Lord Grey, and several other persons of rank
proceeded to meet Mary's forces: their troops
consisted of about eight thousand foot, and two
thousand horse, but so manifest was the fact, that
their cause was unpopular, that Northumberland,
when passing Shoreditch, observed, "see how the
people press to see us, but not one of them saith,
'God speed you.'"[a]   No sooner had he reached
St. Edmond's Bury, than he found his army too
weak to cope with Mary's forces, which amounted
to at least double the number: he therefore wrote
urgently to the Council, desiring reinforcements,
and they gladly availed themselves of the pretext
which the appearance of executing his demands
afforded them of quitting the Tower; but it was
their first thought to concert measures for their
own safety, or, as Hume expresses it, "to shake
off his usurped tyranny." Arundel took the lead

[a] Baker's *Chronicle*, sub anno 1553, p. 313.

in throwing away the cloak which had covered his
real sentiments; and at a meeting which had been
previously appointed to take place at Baynard's
Castle, this nobleman, who with the most contemptible hypocrisy had a few days before boasted
of his readiness to spill his heart's blood in Lady
Jane's cause, now represented Northumberland's
cruelty and injustice, the inordinacy of his ambition, his criminal designs, and the guilt in which he
had involved the whole Council; and he concluded
his address by pointing out, that the only means
which then existed of atoning for their crime, was
by an immediate return to the duty which they
owed to their lawful sovereign.   Pembroke with
ardour seconded the motion, laid his hand on his
sword, and vowed he was ready to fight any man
who expressed a contrary sentiment.   The Mayor
and Aldermen of London were sent for, and Mary
was proclaimed with a zeal and affection, that
formed a striking contrast to the manner in which
the unhappy Jane had been announced a few weeks
preceding.[a]   This important change was effected
about the 19th of July, at which time neither
ambition nor hope could conceal the desperate state
of Lady Jane's situation: Northumberland, however, aware that his fortunes and his life were at

[a] Hume; corroborated by extracts from several contemporary letters.

stake, advanced from Cambridge to Bury, where
finding himself deserted, his cause totally hope-
less, and the general feeling unequivocally expressed in Mary's favour, he at length suffered his
reason to overcome his wishes, and with a mean-
ness no less disgraceful than unavailing, he himself proclaimed Mary, Queen of England. Lloyd
quaintly remarks, that the spectators of his conduct on the occasion, "more believing the grief
in his eyes when they let down tears, than the
joy professed by his hands when he threw up his
cap;" and to the same writer we are indebted for
information of a fact still more humiliating, for
he states, that when the Duke was arrested by
the Earl of Arundel, he fell at his feet and
"craved mercy." Of this nobleman little remains to be said: he was speedily committed to
the Tower, and soon afterwards brought to trial;
and as his treason was displayed in too multiplied
a manner to admit of a question, the only part of
the proceedings worthy of notice is, that when he
implored the mercy of the Court for his children,
he assured them that Lady Jane herself was so
far from aspiring to the Crown, " that she was by
enticement and force made to accept it;" on the
22nd of August following, in pursuance of his sentence, he was executed on Tower-hill, with Sir
John Gates, and Sir Thomas Palmer.

At this crisis in Lady Jane Grey's life, she becomes an object of the deepest interest; and she has been described to have made misery itself amiable by her patient and pious behaviour.[a] The first person who acquainted her with the events which had taken place, is said to have been her father, the Duke of Suffolk; who, entering her chamber, told her she must now divest herself of the royal robes, and be contented to return to a private station: it is stated that she received the information with apparent joy, and assured him she would put them off with infinitely more pleasure than she felt when she assumed them, and which she never would have done, but in obedience to the commands of her mother and himself.[b]

Immediately after Mary became firmly seated on the throne, Lady Jane and her husband, as well as the Duke and Duchess of Suffolk, were confined as state prisoners in the Tower; and the following anecdote proves the rapidity with which the alteration in her situation was effected. A Mr. Edward Underhill, who had been admitted into the Band of Gentlemen Pensioners by Edward VI. was at that time about the person of Jane: in his youth he had been a man of pleasure, but being converted to the Reformed Religion, he be-

[a] Fuller.   [b] Baker.

came so zealous a protestant that his comrades designated him the "Hot-Gospeller;" from these circumstances he became a favorite at the new Court, and was on duty at the Tower when his wife was confined with a son. The baptism of the infant was fixed for the 19th of July, and the Duke of Suffolk and the Earl of Pembroke had consented to stand as sponsors by proxy, and the Lady Jane not only signified her intention of being godmother, but as a still higher mark of favour, desired that the child should be called Guildford, after her husband. The baptism as appointed took place, and Lady Throckmorton wife to Sir Nicholas, was deputed to act as the royal proxy. On leaving the Tower that evening, Lady Throckmorton received the usual commands from Lady Jane herself, according to established etiquette, and conveyed them to the assembly she had just quitted; after the ceremony she returned to the Tower, but her surprise may be imagined on entering the royal apartment to find the canopy of state removed, together with all the other ensigns of royalty: she was, however, soon informed by one of the new officers of the charge which had taken place since her departure in the afternoon; and also that her Lady was a prisoner for high treason, and that she must attend her, but under the weight of a similar charge.ᵃ"   l

ᵃ *Biographia Britannica.*

The command issued by Mary relative to her
prisoners, which probably caused them the greatest
anguish, was that Lady Jane and her husband
should be rigorously confined in distinct apart-
ments, by which she prevented that alleviation of
their misfortunes, which mutual endearments
seldom fail to supply.

Suffolk, though at first arrested, appears to
have obtained his liberty about the 31st of July,
but with an engagement to surrender himself if
he was required to do so. Immediately after Lady
Jane became a prisoner, she was called upon to
deliver to the Marquess of Winchester all the
Crown Jewels; and it has been conjectured, that
under that pretence both she and her husband were
divested of every shilling they possessed.ᵃ On
the 3rd of October, the ceremony of Mary's coronation took place, soon after which, measures
were adopted for the arraignment of Lady Jane
and Lord Guildford Dudley, together with his brothers Lord Ambrose, and Lord Henry Dudley; and
on the 13th of November, their trial commenced,
Lady Jane and her husband having on that morning
been escorted from the Tower to the place appointed for the purpose. Fully sensible of the
uselessness of a defence, they pleaded guilty,
and after sentence of death was pronounced on
each of them, the unfortunate Lady Jane and her

ᵃ *Lady Jane Grey and her Times.*

husband were conducted back to their solitary
abode in the Tower. On this appalling occasion, she is said to have evinced the most perfect coolness and intrepidity, and even to have
offered to her companions in misfortune, that
consolation, of which, from her youth and sex she
might naturally be supposed to have stood in need.
During their return, the public sympathy was
loudly expressed; and the uniform testimony of
historians assures us, that but for the subsequent
attempt of her father, their youth and innocence
would have moved even the unfeminine heart of
Mary, to have preserved their lives.

It was not until the day of their trial, that
Lady Jane and her husband had been allowed to
see each other since the sad change in their fortunes, but on their return to the Tower, they
were again separated. At this period Mary, perhaps disposed to affect a clemency foreign to her
nature, and desirous of commencing her reign with
an act of popularity, pardoned the Marquess of
Northampton and Sir Henry Gates; and ordered
the restraint to which the two illustrious personages had been subjected, to be considerably relaxed.
Lord Guildford and his brother, Lord Ambrose
Dudley, were permitted to walk on the leads of
the Tower, whilst to Lady Jane was conceded the
indulgence of taking exercise in the Queen Gar-

den, with other slight favours, which though perhaps otherwise unimportant, were hailed by their
friends as the harbingers of a speedy and permanent
release.   During her confinement, Fox and other
writers have positively asserted that the Queen
made frequent efforts to convert her to the Catholic
Faith, and they have even gone so far as to state,
that the most solemn promises of life and fortune
were made, if she would yield to their solicitations.
Of the truth of these statements, which are extremely probable, we have now no means of de-
ciding, but to her eternal honor, and doubtless to her immortal advantage, the sin of apostacy
was not her's.   No temporal advantage could persuade her too well regulated mind to forsake its
God; and if the allurements alluded to were really
held out, few have higher pretensions to be ranked
among the martyrs to their faith.   All Lady Jane's
biographers have asserted, that her letter to a noble
friend newly fallen from the truth,ᵃ was addressed
to Dr. Harding, who had been her father's chaplain, but became a convert to the doctrines of the
Catholic church; and they expressly inform us, that
it was written after her condemnation: part of this
statement is however decidedly erroneous, for the
epistle in question was signed with her maiden
name; and as Harding did not declare the change in

ᵃ This letter will be found in a subsequent page.

his sentiments until after Mary's accession, the same
fact proves that it could not have been addressed
to him, unless, as is not improbable, Lady Jane
was acquainted with the alteration in his opinions
some time before he publicly avowed it.   The authenticity of that letter has however been the subject of discussion, and the question is too important
to be allowed to pass unnoticed: that it was received as the genuine production of Lady Jane
Grey, both by Fox and Burnet is certain, but some
modern writers have objected to the probability of
its having been written by her, on account of the
intemperate, and indeed vulgar epithets which it
contains.   It is true that the coarseness of its
language is not consonant to the gentleness and
delicacy which we attribute to her disposition, but
we should ask ourselves whether in estimating the
character of this interesting woman, we do not
forget the period in which she lived, and in the
ardour of our admiration, invest her with a refinement of ideas totally incompatible with the manners
of the times: on the subject of religion, less elegance of expression is to be expected, than on any
other, for in all ages the use of scriptural terms
has been tolerated; and revolting as many of the
epithets certainly are, they were the common
weapons of the reformers of the day, and nearly
the whole of the strong terms used in her letter

are taken from the sacred writings. Religion, in
the middle of the sixteenth century, was far from
a subject which could be discussed with coolness;
and from her peculiar attachment to her faith, she
viewed apostacy with horror, and in the effort
to reclaim the person she addressed, naturally used
expressions contained in the works she had
studied, from their peculiar fitness to describe the
enormity of the crime which he had committed.
We may therefore, without difficulty, imagine
her to have written the objectionable passages
which has produced a doubt on the authenticity of
that celebrated epistle, without its lessening our
esteem for its author.

The warmth with which Mary's pretensions
had been received by the nation abated, when her
attachment to popery became so decided, and her
projected marriage with Philip of Spain excited
great alarm: no sooner was it celebrated, than a
new insurrection was formed, and of which the
ill-fated Lady Jane, ever a sufferer by the folly or
the crimes of others, was destined to be the victim. The discontent of the protestant part of the
community, prompted Sir Thomas Wyatt to attempt to raise the county of Kent, and Sir Peter
Carew that of Devon. The Duke of Suffolk,
whose unaccountable weakness, neither danger
nor experience could correct, seduced by the pros-

pect of once more seeing their imperial diadem on his daughter's brow, joined the conspirators, and undertook to raise the midland counties. Carew's impatience frustrated the little hope of success which existed; his forces were speedily suppressed by the Earl of Bedford, and he himself obliged to fly into France. The moment Suffolk was apprized of this circumstance, the fear of an arrest obliged him to leave London, and he was accompanied in his flight by his brothers, Lord Leonard and Lord Thomas Grey. His immediate object was to raise the counties of Warwick and Leicester, where his influence lay, but he was so closely pursued by the Earl of Huntingdon, that he was obliged to disperse his followers; and being discovered in his concealment, in the park of his mansion of Astley, in Leicestershire, was brought a prisoner to the metropolis. Wyatt's attempt was at first more successful, but his forces were at length routed, and their leader taken prisoner.

No sooner was this rebellion crushed, than it was resolved to carry the sentence which had been passed on Lady Jane Grey into execution, on which Baker quaintly observes, "then was verified the fathers have eaten sour grapes, and the children's teeth are set on edge; the innocent Lady must suffer for her father's fault, for if her father the Duke of Suffolk had not this second time made shipwreck of his

loyalty, his daughter perhaps had never tasted the
salt waters of the Queen's displeasure, but now as a
rock of offence, she is the first that must be removed ;" and on the 8th of February, Feckenham,
the Queen's confessor, was sent to announce to her
the awful tidings, that she must prepare herself
to die on the ensuing day. She received the intimation with resignation, and told Feckenham
that she had long expected it; he then used every
argument of which he was master, to persuade
her to change her religion, and construing her
reply that she had now no time to think of any
thing, but to prepare herself to meet her God by
prayer, into a request that her execution might
be delayed, applied to the Queen who granted her
a reprieve of three days. The desire of making her
a convert to the church of Rome, was in all probability the sole motive of this indulgence, which
Feckenham instantly announced to her; but to his
surprize she mildly observed, "you are much deceived if you think I have any desire of longer
life, for 1 assure you, since the time you
went from me, my life hath been so tedious to
me, that I long for nothing so much as death, and
since it is the Queen's pleasure, I am most willing
to undergo it; neither did I wish the Queen to
be solicited for such a purpose." Her sentiments
having been communicated to Mary, she became

inflamed in an increased degree with the wish to induce Lady Jane to renounce her religion, and under colour of the most tender concern for her eternal welfare, persecuted her with the visits of priests, who disturbed her devotions, and harassed her with constant disputations: so far indeed was the attempt carried, that the offer of a further reprieve was made in order that she might in the time thus afforded, pay what they termed a proper regard to the welfare of her soul. In this trying scene, however, she remained inflexible, and displayed a fortitude never surpassed: conscious of the stability of her faith, she is said to have consented to admit the conference proposed by Feckenham, for the discussion of the subject; but that when the time arrived, she was anxious to avoid the controversy, observing, that she had no time to spare; that disputation might be fit for the living, but not for the dying, and that therefore the surest sign of his having that compassion for her of which he made such strong professions, would be to leave her undisturbed in making her peace with God; but, actuated by the wish to display his powers both before the clergy, by whom he was accompanied, and the individuals who had been purposely admitted, he refused to comply with her request. How far this account may be received as correct is doubtful, for in the introduction to this "Conference," printed in a scarce tract,[a] the following statement is prefixed, and which may be considered as the most probable cause of the dialogue having been preserved.

"Divers learned Romish Catholics, and even those which were of the best fame and reputation, were sent unto her to dissuade her from that true profession of the Gospel, which from her cradle she had ever held; each striving by art, by flattery, by threatenings, by promise of life, or what else might move most in the bosom of a weak woman, who should become master of so great and worthy a prize; but all their labours were bootless, for she had art to confound their art, wisdom to withstand their wisdom, resolution above their menaces, and such a true knowledge of life, that death was to her no other than a most familiar acquaintance; in the end, a deep read divine called M. Feckenham, then Chaplain to Queen Mary, was sent unto her about some four days before her death, who had with her a long and tedious disputation, but, as the rest, found himself in all holy gifts so short of her excellence, that he acknowledged himself fitter to be her disciple than teacher, and thereupon humbly besought her to

[a] *The Life, Death, and Actions of the Most Chaste, Learned, and Religious Lady, the Lady Jane Grey, &c.* London, 1615.

deliver unto him some brief sum of her faith,
which he might hereafter keep, and as a faithful
witness publish to the world; to which she willingly condescended, and bad him boldly question her
in what points of religion so ever it pleased him,
and she would give her faithful and believing answer, such as she would ever be ready to seal
with her dearest blood."

This account differs very materially from that
of an anonymous writer,[a] as well as from the
statement which follows the above, in the same
pamphlet, where it is said that the argument took
place publicly, before an assemblage of the noble
and learned, when Feckenham, by his coarseness
and brutality, lost the respect of his auditors; but
this appears highly improbable, from the internal
evidence afforded by the dialogue itself, and by
the consideration that it is evidently what it is
described to be in the preceding extract, "a brief
sum of her faith which he might hereafter keep;"
and its being in a catechetical form is well explained, by her having requested him "boldly to
question her in what points of religion so ever it
pleased him." Moreover it would be difficult to
reconcile its having been signed by herself on any
other grounds; for if her sentiments had been
merely verbally expressed, as must be inferred

<hr>

[a] Reprinted in "*The Phœnix*," No. xviii. Vol. II. p. 27.

from the narrative given by the writers just cited, its having ever existed as a document attested by her own signature, cannot well be explained.

In estimating the conduct of Feckenham, we must remember that the unfavourable descriptions of his conduct towards Lady Jane Grey are handed down to us from most prejudiced sources; a martyrologist is never an impartial biographer of a priest of the religion which produced the immolation of those whose virtues he records; and judging of Mary's chaplain by perhaps the only positive evidence which exists—the interesting dialogue before us—the conclusion which it allows is, by no means what his enemies have represented.[a]

[a] It has been said, that "when he called to take his last leave of Lady Jane, he could not refrain from the cruel taunt of 'Madam, I am sorry for you and your obstinacy, and now I am assured that you and I shall never meet again:' and that she replied, 'it is most true, Sir, we shall never meet again, except God turn your heart; for I stand undoubtedly assured, that unless you repent and turn to God, you are in a sad and desperate case, and I pray to God to send you his holy spirit, for he hath given you his great gift of utterance, if it please him to open the eyes of your heart to his truth.' Feckenham, more enraged at this, turned rudely upon his heel, and left her without obeisance, whilst she, like a suffering saint, withdrew herself into her bed-chamber to meditation and prayer." Whatever bigotry is to be found in the observation imputed to Feckenham, it

The respite offered by the Queen was, notwithstanding its refusal by Lady Jane, confirmed by the Council, and she consequently lived to be aware that her father was brought to the same prison, for the purpose of undergoing a similar fate. That she was not acquainted with his pre-.vious arrest, is inferred from her having written her celebrated letter to him, which is inserted among her other works towards the end of the volume.

It was on Saturday the 10th of February, 1554, that the Duke of Suffolk, together with Lord John Grey his brother, were conveyed to the Tower; and the Monday following was appointed for the execution of Lady Jane and her husband Lord Guildford Dudley. The last evening of her life was employed by her in religious duties: having taken up a Greek Testament, and attentively perused it for some time, she discovered a few pages of clean paper at the end of the volume, " which, as it were awakening and inciting her zeal to some good and charitable office, she took her pen, and in those waste leaves wrote a most godly and learned exhortation" to

must be confessed that there is not a little acrimony in the retort : but every thing which flows from a spring so poisoned by prejudice as the pen of the author of a martyrology, must, as is observed in the text, be received with great hesitation.

her sister Katherine.   Such is the motive to which
the letter to her sister, which is reprinted in this
volume, has been attributed; but affection and
a natural desire that the important subject, then
uppermost in her thoughts, should also employ the
attention of a beloved relative, more rationally ex-
plains the inducement which prompted her to leave
so solemn a memorial of her regard.   This letter
is of the highest interest, and displays the perfect
self-possession of its lovely writer in the most satisfactory light: it likewise affords a lesson no less
impressive than essential, for it teaches us the
powerful solace which religion bestowed in so mo-
mentous an hour.   In the narrative which follows
this letter in the pamphlet before cited, it is
asserted that she was destined, even on the
last evening of her existence, to be harassed
by new persecutions from the Catholic divines;
for no sooner had she finished her letter than
two bishops, with some other priests entered her
chamber, and employed more than two hours in
the effort to convert her; but her strength of mind
remained unimpaired, and we are thus presented
with a splendid example of female constancy and
firmness in a girl, who had not then attained her
seventeenth year.   Her tormenters, worn out by a
resolution which no arguments could shake, left
her as they styled it, in her obstinacy; though it

is said that she was not permitted to pass the brief
space of her existence which remained, without
experiencing similar attempts.   It was also on this
evening that she finished and corrected the prayer,
which is likewise inserted in this volume.

The fatal morning at length arrived: it was
originally intended that Lady Jane and Lord Guildford should suffer together on Tower Hill, but
the Council dreading the effect of their youth
and innocence on the populace, changed their
orders; and it was therefore determined that Lord
Guildford only should be executed on that spot,
and that Lady Jane's death should take place within
the verge of the Tower.   Guildford, on the morning of his execution, urgently requested to be
allowed to bid a last adieu to the cherished partner of his heart, and although his wishes were
not refused by the Queen, the gratification of them
was denied him by Lady Jane : her strong judgment
at once dreaded the effects of an interview, that was
likely to overwhelm them with unavailing sorrow,
and thus to destroy that firmness which was so
necessary to enable them to bear the trying scene
with composure : she reminded him that their separation would be but for a moment, and that they
would soon rejoin each other, where their affec-
tions would be united for ever, and where neither
misfortunes, disappointments, nor death could

reach them, but where their felicity would be
eternal! Lord Guildford was first led to his fate,
and when passing under the window of his wife, obtained one last token of her love and remembrance.
What tale of sorrow it may be asked, has ever
equalled this heart rending scene? But her cup
of bitterness was not yet full, for besides her own
bodily sufferings, she experienced the agony of
seeing the headless corpse of her husband conveyed from the place of his execution. The manner in which this appalling sight met her view
has been differently stated; in the narrative inserted in the tract before noticed,[a] it is said that
she encountered it on her way to the scaffold; whilst
Mr. Howard, her latest biographer, follows those
writers who assert that when sitting in her apartment awaiting the awful summons, she heard the
cart pass under her window, and rose notwithstanding the efforts of her attendants to restrain
her. This account is not so probable as the other,
for she would scarcely have sought so dreadful
a spectacle; and as she had carefully avoided an
interview with him, lest their firmness might have
been destroyed, it cannot be believed that she
would willingly view an object still more calculated

[a] *Life, Death, and Actions of the Most Chaste, Learned,
and Religious Lady, the Lady Jane Grey.*

to disturb her thoughts.[a] Dudley we are told exhibited considerable dignity and fortitude; after some time spent in prayer, he addressed the assembled multitude, merely to request them to pray for him, and placing his head on the block, it was in a few seconds separated from his body.

So soon as the closing scene of Lord Guildford's life was over, the Sheriffs announced to Lady Jane that they were ready to attend her to the scaffold: nor did this awful summons shake the fortitude which she had displayed throughout her imprisonment. The pamphlet which has been frequently cited,[b] describes her conduct on the occasion in the following words: "and being come down and delivered into the hands of the Sheriffs, they might behold in her countenance so gravely settled with all modest and comely resolution,

[a] Grafton corroborates the statement that Lady Jane's meeting the mutilated body of her husband was entirely accidental, for he says, Lord Guildford Dudley's "dead carkas liyng in a Carre in strawe was againe brought into the Tower, at the same instant that the Ladie Iane his wife went to her death within the Tower, which miserable sight was to her a double sorrow and griefe."

Grafton it must be remembered was contemporary with the event here described.

[b] *Life, Death, and Actions of the most Chaste, Learned, and Religious Lady, the Lady Jane Grey*, and which appears to have been copied in the *Phœnix*, No. xviii.

that not the least hair or mote either of fear or
grief could be perceived to proceed either out of
her speech or motions, but like a demure body
going to be united to her heart's best and longest
beloved; so shewed she forth all the beams of a
well mixt and temporal alacrity, rather instruct-
ing patience how it should suffer, than being by
patience any way able to endure the travel of so
grievous a journey: with this blessed and modest
boldness of spirit, undaunted and unaltered she
went towards the scaffold." She was conducted
to the place of execution by Sir John Brydges, the
Lieutenant of the Tower, and was entirely occupied in the perusal of a book of prayers, though
Fox asserts, that her devotions were continually
interrupted by Feckenham. On reaching the scaffold, she mounted it without hesitation, and addressed the assembled crowd in a short speech, in
which she admitted her crime against the Queen,
but protested that she was innocent either of
wishing or procuring the royal dignity: and
after requesting those who heard her to bear witness that she died a true Christian woman, and
that she expected salvation only through the
mercy of God, in the merits of the blood of his
son Jesus Christ, she confessed that when she
did know the word of God, she neglected it, and
loved herself, and that therefore the punishment

had happily and worthily happened to her for her
sins; she thanked God for his goodness for giving
her time to repent, and concluded her speech by
requesting them to assist her with their prayers.[a]
She then knelt down, and addressing Feckenham,
asked if she should say the Psalm of *Misereri Mei
Deus*, to which he assented, and she repeated it in
English, in the most devout manner. When it
was concluded, she arose and began to prepare
herself for her fate, by giving Mrs. Tylney, one
of her maids, her gloves and handkerchief, and her
book to Mr. Thomas Brydges, the Lieutenant's
brother; and proceeding to untie her gown, the
executioner offered to assist her, but she requested
him to let her alone; and turning towards her gen-
tlewomen, who helped her in taking it off, together
with her "Frose paste,[a] and neckecher," they gave
her a handkerchief to tie round her eyes. The

---

[a] A copy of the speech will be found in p. 51.

[b] Though very considerable pains have been taken to
ascertain the precise meaning of the article so described,
they were without success. It was evidently something worn
near the neck, and was possibly from its name of German
origin. Various and ingenious as the conjectures are with
which the author has been favoured on the subject, he is
rather inclined to coincide with that of a literary friend,
that it was a species of tucker which covered the neck;
and that it was probably called, "Fronts-piece."

executioner now fell on his knees and begged her forgiveness, which she most willingly granted him; and he requested her to stand upon the straw, on approaching which the block met her view, but the sight of it did not in the least affect her resolution, and she merely requested him to dispatch her quickly. She then, again knelt and asked, "will you take it off before I lay me down," and being answered in the negative, she tied the handkerchief before her eyes, and felt for the block, observing, "what shall I do? where is it?" One of the by-standers immediately guided her, when she laid her head on it, and stretching forth her body, exclaimed, "Lord, into thy hands I commend my spirit,"—immediately the axe fell;—and the world, closed for ever on one of the most interesting women that ever adorned it![a]

It is a singular fact, that numerous as the biographers of Lady Jane Grey have been, not

[a] The account of the execution of Lady Jane Grey, is chiefly taken from a reprint in the Archæologia, Vol. xiii. p. 406, from "an exceedingly rare, if not unique printed tract, not noticed either by Ames or Herbert, one part of which is entitled 'The ende of the Lady Jane upon the Scaffolde,' it is without date, but contains internal evidence of having been printed immediately after that event, in the first year of the reign of Queen Mary." It differs in a very slight degree from the narrative of Fox.

one of them has alluded to the interment of her body; and it is equally extraordinary that no monument of so celebrated a character, or of her husband should exist. The presumption is, that they were both buried in the chapel of the Tower, but the historian of that fortress * has not been able to find any conclusive evidence of the place where their remains were deposited. Thus, whilst tombs have been erected, not only by the hands of private friendship, but from public esteem, and even by royal command, to perpetuate the names of individuals of much less importance, as well as of inferior moral worth, the ashes of two illustrious victims to state policy, in one of whom to royal birth, was united every virtue which renders the female sex estimable, have been allowed to moulder in obscurity! That in the present age, when the spirit of inquiry has produced the exhumation of several of the celebrated dead, some pains should not have been taken to ascertain where the bodies of Lady Jane Grey and her husband were interred, not from mere motives of curiosity, but from the better feeling of removing their remains to the tombs of their ancestors, and of erecting a monument to their memory, cannot but be a subject of surprize.

* John Bayley, Esq. F.R.S. F.S.A.

Mr. Howard,[a] and almost every other biographer of Lady Jane, has stated that when she descended from her room to go to the scaffold, she presented Sir John Gage, the Lieutenant of the Tower, in compliance with his request that she would bestow on him some small present which he might keep as a memorial of her, with her table book, in which she had just written three sentences on seeing her husband's dead body.   One of these sentences we are informed, was in Greek, one in Latin, and the third in English; and the purport of them was, that human justice was against his body, but the divine mercy would be favourable to his soul; that if her own fault deserved punishment, yet her youth at least, and her imprudence, were worthy of excuse, and that God and posterity she trusted, would shew her favor.   The whole of this story, however, is not only improbable, but it is not supported by a shadow of evidence; and still more, many circumstances tend to convince us of its entire fallacy.

If she really wrote the sentences in question, the assertion that she saw the body of her husband from her chamber window, instead of her having accidentally met it on her way to the scaffold, is confirmed; and as very much depends whether such was the fact, it is important to inquire into

[a] *Lady Jane Grey and Her Times*, p. 379.

the truth of it. It has been before observed, that independently of the improbability of her seeking an object so calculated to excite her feelings, Grafton, who was nearly contemporary with the event, informs us that the body of Lord Guildford Dudley lying in a car in straw, was brought into the Tower " at the same instant in which Lady Jane went to her death, within the Tower ;" this statement is likewise followed in the tract reprinted in the Phœnix, as well as in the pamphlet which has been so often cited.

Hence, the most probable account is consonant to the representations of more than one writer ; and it may with confidence be asked, whether it can for a moment be believed that a young and amiable girl, who on numerous occasions evinced that she was endowed with even more than her sex's usual delicacy and softness, would at any moment have written epigrams on the mutilated corpse of her husband, especially whether she would have done so within a few seconds after she had seen so ghastly a spectacle, and when even she herself was expecting a momentary summons to undergo a similar fate? That she possessed an extraordinary firmness of character is certain ; but the female who could have done what has been held up to the world as a subject of admiration, must have been little less than a monster ; and instead of the esteem, would most

justly have deserved the execration of posterity.
But it is certain, not only from the testimony of the
writers alluded to, but from other circumstances,
that she was incapable of such horrible conduct;
and so far from writing epigrams on her ill-fated
husband, we are told, what nature and a knowledge
of the female heart at once suggest must have
been the case, that when she beheld Lord Guildford's corpse, "so miserable a sight was to her a
double sorrow and grief;"[a] and according to another
writer, "the spectacle a little startled her, and
many tears were seen to descend and fall upon her
cheeks."[b] Of the lives which have been written
of Lady Jane Grey, perhaps the one most deserving
of credit is that by Florio, and though he states that
in compliance with the wish of the governor of the
Tower, she wrote passages somewhat similar to
those attributed to her on her husband, yet he informs us that they were on *herself;* his account is,

"Jvanzi ch'ella (cioe Giovanna Graia) fusse
condotta alla preparata manara, fu ricercata dal
governatore di Torre, a lasciar li alcuna memoria
di lei, a cio stringendolo la molta affettione, che le
portava, et essa fattosi dare un picol libretto, vi
scrisse sopra tre sentenze: una Greca, una Latina,

---

[a] Grafton before quoted, p. lxxxix.
[b] Phœnix, No. 42.

et una Inglese, lequali erano in questa sostanza.
La Greca era tale : la morte dara la pena al mio
corpo del fallo, ma la mia anima giustificare inanzi
al conspetto di Dio la innocenza mia. La Latina
diceva : Se la giustitia ha luogo nel mio corpo, la-
nima mia l'havera nella misericordia di Dio. L
Inglese : il fallo è degno di morte, ma il modo di
mia ignoranza doveva meritar pietà, et escusatione
appresso il mondo, et alle leggi.[a] Florio's relation was apparently copied by an English writer
of the last century, who observes, "As she was
brought out, the Lieutenant of the Tower desired
her to favour him with some commemorative memorial, upon which she asked for her table book
and wrote three short sentences, in Greek, Latin,
and English, by which she asserted her innocency,
declaring that if her fault deserved punishment,
her youth at least and her ignorance were excuse-
able, and that God and posterity would shew her
favour."[b]

Notwithstanding the repeated assertion, that
sentences or epigrams, either on her husband or
herself, were written by Lady Jane, it appears

[a] Historia de la Vita e de la Morte de l'Illustriss. Sig-
nora Giovanna Graia, &c. de l'Authore M. Michelangelo
Florio. 1607. pp. 134-135.

[b] *The Life, Character, and Death of the Most Illustrious
Pattern of Female Virtue, the Lady Jane Grey.* 1714. 8vo.

o

to be at least questionable, whether such was
actually the case. It has, it is presumed, been
proved that they were never composed upon
her husband; and though it is not in the least
improbable that she should have expressed such
sentiments about herself, or indeed relative to
him, at any other period, it is totally repugnant to
the feelings with which we may suppose her to
have been possessed when proceeding to her execution, that if solicited at so awful a moment for
some memorial to keep for her sake, instead of
hastily bestowing on the supplicant some trifling
article which she had about her person, she should
have calmly called for her memorandum book, pen
and ink, with the object of displaying her literary
attainments.   If the sentences were written, it is
singular that copies of them should not be extant, even if the original book in which they are
said to have been inserted has been lost; nothing,
however, but an account of the subject of each of
them has been preserved; and this fact, together
with the following circumstances, as well as those
which have just been stated, confirm the suspicion that the epigrams in question never existed.
From the narrative of each of the writers who
have been alluded to, it would appear that two
books were given by Lady Jane Grey; that in
these she wrote three sentences at the request, in

both instances, of the Lieutenant of the Tower, who
in some places is called Sir John Brydges, and in
others Sir John Gage: and that one of these books
was a table book, and the other a prayer book.
The only positive proof on this point which can now
be adduced, is with respect to the latter, because
it is at this moment in the British Museum, and in
which, a sentence in the autograph of Lady Jane
expressly professes to have been written at the request of the Lieutenant of the Tower, who at that
time was Sir John Brydges, whilst Sir John Gage
was the constable of that fortress; and in all
probability it was this book which she gave on the
scaffold to Mr. Thomas Brydges, the Lieutenant's
brother. Few families have had such accomplished
biographers as those of Brydges[a] and Gage,[b] but
no information on the subject is given by either of
them, nor is the existence of such "table book" to
be traced. In what manner the book given to Sir
John Brydges came into the Harleian collection

[a] Sir Egerton Brydges, Bart. K. J.; the numerous literary productions of this elegant writer are too well known,
and too highly appreciated, to require any comment.

[b] John Gage, Esq. of Lincoln's Inn, Barrister at Law,
F.R.S. F.S.A. whose "History and Antiquities of Hea-
grave, in Suffolk," 4to. 1822, is, beyond all comparison,
the most interesting family history that has ever issued from
the press.

does not appear, but from the similarity of the causes which are said to have been Lady Jane's motive for writing those sentences; the constant confusion of writers relative to Sir John Brydges and Sir John Gage, which seems to have arisen from its having been always intended to describe the Lieutenant, instead of the Constable of the Tower; the positive proof of the correctness of one account, and the absence of every kind of evidence, of the truth of the other, combine to persuade us that only one book, namely, that which is now in the British Museum, was ever written in by Lady Jane Grey at the request of a third person, in the manner which has been related.

This long digression will not, it is hoped, be deemed unnecessary: to the admirers of this distinguished woman, every action of her life, and especially every occurrence in the last hour of her existence is of the deepest interest; whilst to those who employ their own minds in the discrimination of character, it was important, that what cannot but have appeared an anomaly in her conduct, should be investigated; and if what has been said tends to create a suspicion of the truth of the unfeminine action imputed to her, even if it does not prove that it never took place, it will not have been written in vain. The inquiry was also called for, because it relates to the authenticity of certain articles which have been attributed to her pen; and although that subject has been noticed in the preface, still the question of the genuineness of these epigrams is too much connected with other circumstances to have been there discussed with advantage.

Fuller asserts, that it was reported at the time of Lady Jane's death, that she was in the most interesting situation in which a married woman can be placed; and observes, "cruelty to cut down the tree with blossoms on it; and that which hath saved the lives of many women, hastened her death;" but, he adds, "God only knows the truth thereof." The same circumstance is noticed by Sir Thomas Chaloner in his well known elegy; but the point has never been determined, and as is well observed in the *Biographia Britannica*, "whereas some of our own writers seem to doubt whether Lady Jane was with child or not at the time of her decease, and foreigners have improved this into a direct assertion that she was five months gone; it seems to be improbable, since there were at that time so many busy and inquisitive people, that if the fact had been true, it must have been known, and would have been perpetually repeated in those pieces that were every day sent abroad, in order to exasperate the nation against the Queen and her ministers." Upon so delicate a question, any conjecture would at this

period be ridiculous, and as there does not appear
to be the least possibility of arriving at a satisfactory conclusion, it would be useless to enter into
any discussion on the subject.

A very interesting circumstance connected
with Lady Jane Grey, occurred a few years since
on making some alterations in the Tower: on
converting an apartment in Beauchamp's Tower,
which had formerly been the place in which state
prisoners were confined, into a mess room for the
officers of the garrison there, several inscriptions
were discovered on the walls of the room. They
appeared to have been made with nails, or some
other pointed instrument, and the greater part of
them were undoubtedly the autographs of the unfortunate tenants of the place. Amongst them,
was the word

IANE . IANE

and which, it has been conjectured, was written
by herself, and that some latent meaning was contained in the repetition of her signature, by which
she at once styled herself a Queen, and intimated
that not even the horrors of a prison would force
her to relinquish that title.[a] This suggestion is
not, however, entitled to any consideration, for independently of its having been proved that she was

[a] *Archæologia*, Vol. xiii. p. 70, communicated by the
Rev. John Brand, Secretary to the Society of Antiquaries

placed in a different apartment from that where
this inscription was found, her character and conduct render it extremely unlikely that motives of
vanity should have had any place in her wounded
mind. Another antiquary has supposed that it
was written by her father in-law, the Duke of Northumberland; but the most rational idea which has
been suggested on the subject is that of Mr.
Bayley,* who considers it to have been inscribed
by her unhappy partner, Lord Guildford Dudley;
for nothing is more probable than that in his separation from his wife, he should have solaced
himself by marking the walls of his prison with her
name. If it could be proved that it was traced
by his hand, so affecting a memorial would speak
eloquently of his tenderness, and we might feel con-
vinced that the affection which has been attributed
to this interesting pair unquestionably existed.

A curious engraving in a similar manner, by
the Duke of Northumberland whilst in confinement,
is also deserving of notice. It exhibited the device of that once powerful nobleman, and contained
within a square, each side of which was about twenty
inches long, a bear with a collar and chain, and a
lion, the supporters of his arms, holding a ragged
staff, the ancient cognizance of the Earls of Warwick; they were surrounded by a border composed

* *History of the Tower.*

of a foliage of roses, acorns, and apparently lilies ; under the animals was his name,

IOHN DVDLI.

beneath which were the following lines,

YOW THAT THESE BEASTS DO WEL BEHOLDE AND SE,
MAY DEME WITHE EASE WHEREFORE HERE MADE THEY BE
WITHE BORDERS EKE WHEREIN *by those is found*
A BROTHERS NAMES WHO LIST TO SERCHE THE GROVND.

There is much difficulty in comprehending the meaning which the illustrious prisoner intended to convey by these lines and the device.   It has been supposed, that a pun was meant, as the *roses* easily separate themselves in the division of his brother Ambrose's christian name,[a] whilst Mr. Howard remarks, that he evidently punned upon his own misfortunes, and his brother Ambrose's name.[b]   Neither of these conjectures appear to be strictly correct, and the following, in the absence of a more satisfactory explanation, is submitted.   The third line which was either unfinished or had been partly defaced, has not, it is presumed, any connection with the last line; in all probability it stated that the border of roses alluded to the name of his son Ambrose, and it is not impossible but that the acorns and other flowers

[a] *Archæologia,* Vol. xiii. p. 70.
[b] *Lady Jane Grey and Her Times,* p. 319.

bore some allusion to the cognizances or symbols of
his other children, who were at the same time confined in the Tower; namely, John, Earl of Warwick, his eldest son, and the Lords Ambrose,
Guildford, and Henry Dudley, his younger sons,
though from the imperfect manner in which they
were sculptured, and our ignorance of their each
having adopted some particular cognizance or
badge, nothing certain can be determined on the
subject. The third line admits of a different in-
terpretation, for the idea that his *brother's* name
was meant by the roses, is at once set aside by the
simple fact that the Duke of Northumberland never
had a brother called Ambrose. His only brothers
were Andrew and Henry, the former of whom, Sir
Andrew Dudley, Knight of the Garter,* was at

* It does not appear at what time he received the honor
of Knighthood, but in 1551 he obtained a grant of the manor
of Whitney, by the style of Sir Andrew Dudley, Knight.
On 23 April, 5 Edw. VI. 1552, he was elected a Knight of the
Garter, and in October following, upon being recalled from
the Castle of Guisnes of which he was Captain, he was appointed gentleman of the King's Privy Chamber, and was soon
afterwards nominated Keeper of the Palace of Westminster,
and Master of the Wardrobe. He joined in the attempt of his
brother, the Duke of Northumberland, to place Lady Jane
on the throne, and was condemned to death as a traitor
the 19 August, 1553, but was reprieved, and having been
pardoned, was discharged from the Tower, 18 October, 1554;

that moment his fellow prisoner for the same
crime, and who in all likelihood was alluded to in
the last line; for no pun can be deemed too bar-
barous if it will explain a device of the times.

A brother's names who list to search the ground,

may be understood to mean, that as the border
contained the names of his sons, his brother's names
would be discovered by searching the ground on
which his *hand drew* the lines and device that pre-
ceded it; this, however, will only give a pun on
his baptismal name AN-DREW, but as the expression
is "a brother's names," we must suppose the word
DUDLEY to be supplied by the person who *searches
the ground* for the solution of the riddle, exclaim-
ing, "*Dudley's hand drew*, this," and we shall at
once have ANDREW DUDLEY. This conjecture will
doubtlessly be considered "far-fetched," but those
who are accustomed to the quaint devices of the
period, will not perhaps think it destitute of probability. The two first lines

You that these beasts do well behold and see,
May deem with ease wherefore here made they be.

alluded to his device of the lion, bear, and ragged
staff, by which he represented himself; and he

the remainder of his life he passed in privacy at his house in
Tothill Street, where he died in 1559. *Biographia Britannia.*

justly observes, that the spectator may easily guess
why they are introduced, namely, to explain his
having been a tenant of that apartment: the roses
are presumed to have been emblematical of his sons,
and the lily was, possibly, allegorical of his beauteous
daughter in-law, Lady Jane, whilst the last line,
it is here conjectured, was allusive to his brother;
thus, by this device a memorial was formed of all his
kindred who were at that time confined in the Tower.
If, however, it be insisted that the allusion in the
last line was to Ambrose Dudley, it can only be
explained by supposing the device to have been
drawn, not as has always been supposed by John,
Duke of Northumberland, but by his eldest son
John Dudley, who was styled Earl of Warwick,
and who, as is before stated, was also committed
to the Tower. He survived his father but a few
months, having died without issue, on the 21 October, 1554, in the twenty-fourth year of his age.[a]

Before concluding this memoir of Lady Jane
Grey, the remarks of Lord Orford on the defects
in her title to the throne merit a short notice; es-
pecially as her father's first marriage with Lady
Katherine Fitz Alan, daughter of the Earl of
Arundel, alluded to in a former page,[b] forms one
of the objections noticed by that celebrated writer.
It is very observable, he remarks, how many de-

[a] *Biog. Britann.*   [b] Page xi.

fects concurred in the title of this princess to the crown. 1.—Her descent was from the younger sister of Henry VIII. and there were descendants of the elder living, whose claim had indeed been set aside by the power given by Parliament to king Henry to regulate the succession; but a power which, not being founded on national expedience, could be of no force; and which was additionally invalidated by that king having, by the same authority, settled the crown preferably on his own daughters, who were now both living. 2.—Her mother, from whom alone Jane could derive any right, was alive. 3.— That mother was young enough to have other children (not being past thirty-one at the death of king Edward VI.) and if she had borne a son, his right, prior to that of his sister, was incontestible. 4.—Charles Brandon, father of the Duchess of Suffolk, had married one woman while contracted to another; but was divorced to fulfil his promise: the repudiated wife was living when he married Mary, queen of France, by whom he had the Duchess. 5.—If, however, Charles Brandon's first marriage should still be deemed null, there is no such plea to be made in favour of the Duchess Frances herself, since Henry, Duke of Suffolk, the father of Jane, was actually married to the sister of the Earl of Arundel, whom he

divorced without the least grounds, in order to
make room for his marriage with Frances, the
mother of Jane.

The first point has been already so fully discussed,[a] that little remains to be said on it.   By
the usual rules of descent of the crown, the issue
of the elder sister would have had an undisputed
claim before those of the younger sister; but as
the legislature had given Henry VIII. power to
regulate the succession by his will, so long as
that act remained unrepealed, it is absurd to argue
that it was of no force;[b] hence the only circumstance worthy of attention is, that under the
will of that monarch, as well as by the statute 35
Hen. VIII. by which power was given to him to
limit the descent of the crown by his Will or by
Letters Patent, his own daughters were named before Lady Jane, and that, at the time of her succession they were both living.   This objection,
though in our view of the subject insurmountable,
might have worn a different complexion in the

[a] Page xxvi. *et seq.*

[b] On the power given to Henry the Eighth to dispose of the crown by his Will or by his Letters Patent, Sir
William Blackstone observes, "a vast power; but notwithstanding, as it was regularly vested in him by the supreme
legislative authority, *it was therefore indisputably valid.*"
Commentaries, Book I. Cap. iii. p. 206.

estimation of her partizans, from the circumstance
that both the daughters of Henry the Eighth had
been bastardized by statute 28 Hen. VIII. and
although by a subsequent act, viz. 35 Hen. VIII.[*]
they were rendered legitimate, and included in the
limitation of the descent of the crown, still the fact
of their having once been solemnly declared incapable of inheriting it, was very important, and it
was naturally seized upon as grounds for urging the
pretensions of Lady Jane Grey ; for, as it has been
already observed, she was, agreeably to the will of
Henry the Eighth, next in succession to the royal
dignity, after the demise of Edward VI. and his
sisters Mary and Elizabeth, without issue.   Hence
it is manifest, that had the two princesses died
before their brother without issue, or what would
have been the same in effect, if they were considered illegitimate, Lady Jane would on the death
of Edward, in 1553, have had fair pretensions to the
throne, not certainly according to the usual descent
of the royal dignity, but according to the provisions
of Henry the Eighth's testament.

The second objection is not for one moment,
tenable : it is evident that Lord Orford has fallen
into the error of nearly every historian, of consider-

* The statutes relating to the succession to the crown,
and likewise Henry the Eighth's testament are more fully
noticed at the end of the volume.

ing that Lady Jane's mother had a prior right to the
throne to her daughter; but it has been before stated,
that Lady Jane Grey had no pretensions whatever
to the crown whilst issue remained of Henry the
Eighth's eldest sister, excepting under the provisions of that monarch's will, and from which her
mother, the Duchess of Suffolk, could derive no
claim, the limitation being, to the issue of her body.[a]

The third objection is equally invalid : for if
the provision of Henry's will, that the crown was
on a certain contingency to vest in the issue of the
Duchess of Suffolk, was acted upon, whenever that
contingency happened, the first person within the
limitation would undoubtedly succeed, notwithstanding the possibility of the birth of a son who
would have a prior claim.   Thus, as the Duchess of
Suffolk had no son living at the death of Edward VI.
and as the crown was entailed, failing her issue
male, on her eldest daughter, if it be conceded that
such son would then have had a right to it, Lady
Jane Grey must have had precisely the same pretensions as would have been possessed by her brother,
had one been in existence.   What would have been
the effect if her succession to the royal dignity had
been undisputed, and her mother had afterwards
given birth to a male infant is another question,
and one which it is not necessary to discuss.

[a] See page xxvii.

Lord Orford's fourth objection is more material than either of the preceding. The manner in which Charles Brandon, Duke of Suffolk, Lady Jane's maternal grandfather, was divorced from his wife Margaret, daughter of John, Marquess Montague, and widow of Sir John Mortimer, Knight, cannot perhaps be precisely ascertained; and on the subject of his marriages, the statements of Dugdale and his other biographers are not quite correct. So soon as he became a favorite with Henry VIII. his royal master availed himself of every occasion to advance his interests: about 1513, he was contracted to Elizabeth Grey, daughter and heir of John Grey, Viscount Lisle, who was then very young, and on the 15 May following, he was in consequence of that alliance created Viscount Lisle; but on coming of age she refused to complete the engagement, and the patent for that dignity was therefore cancelled. Dugdale asserts, that his first wife was Ann, daughter of Sir Anthony Brown, Knight, and his second Margaret, widow of Sir John Mortimer above mentioned; but in his account of the Brandon family,[a] he takes no notice of his contract with Elizabeth Grey, though in another part of his baronage,[b] he says, that she was " either married or was designed to be married to

---

[a] Tome ii. p. 299, et seq.   [b] Tome i. p. 722.

Sir Charles Brandon, by means whereof he had the
title of Viscount Lisle granted to him, and the
heirs male of her body to be begotten by him."
At what time he married Lady Mortimer does not
appear, nor are we informed of the manner in
which he was divorced from her; but it is positively
affirmed that she was living after his,marriage with
the Queen Dowager of France. It seems, however, sufficient to remark the improbability of
his daring to ally himself to the sister of the
reigning monarch, had any circumstance existed
which could render the validity of that contract at
all a subject of suspicion; hence, as his marriage
with the French Queen was fully acknowledged at
the period when it took place, both by his royal
brother in-law and by the nation; and as in a discussion on the subject of the succession in Parliament, anno 13 Eliz. in reference to a charge
of bastardy brought against Lady Frances and
Lady Eleanor Brandon, the Duke's daughters by
the Queen of France, by their illegitimate sister
Lady Powis, it was declared that the point of the
legality of that marriage had been fully settled both
by the laws of the realm and by the canon laws, [a]
it is almost absurd, after the lapse of above two
centuries, to entertain a doubt on the subject. We

[a] Cottonian MSS. Julius F. vi.   Printed in the *Biographia Britannica.*

may therefore safely conclude, that whatever the
nature of the Duke of Suffolk's alliance with Lady
Mortimer might have been, the connection was not
at the time considered to be any impediment to his
marriage with the king's sister, for if the contrary
was the case, we must believe that Henry the
Eighth was aware that his sister was living in open
adultery with one of his own subjects!

The fifth and last defect in Lady Jane Grey's
title, pointed out by his lordship, is scarcely more
important than the preceding, and may be answered
by nearly the same arguments. Although it is
certain that Henry Grey, Duke of Suffolk, had been
either married or contracted to Katherine Fitz
Alan, daughter of the Earl of Arundel, and notwithstanding that it has been stated[a] that the Earl
settled an annuity on her for life; that she survived
him several years; and that her brother William,
Earl of Arundel, was exceedingly displeased at her
having been repudiated; still it must be presumed,
that whatever measures were taken on the occasion, they were deemed to be so entirely efficacious
as to have enabled him to marry again. The object
of the divorce was of course to increase his political
importance by an alliance with the blood royal; but
can we suppose that he would have presumed to ask

[a] " *Dialogue touching the Succession,*" and *MS. Barona-
gium,* cited in the *Biographia Britannica.*

the hand of the king's niece, if he had then a
lawful wife living? or even if he had dared to do
so, can an idea more ridiculous be entertained than
that such a proposition should be acceded to, either
by her royal uncle or by her parents? However
desirable the union might have appeared to the
Marquess of Dorset, it could not possibly have
been so essential to the interests of the Duke and
Duchess of Suffolk as to have induced them to con-
nive at their daughter's dishonor: nor would a subject have been permitted to have allied himself so
nearly to the blood royal, as to render it possible
that the crown might become vested in his descendants, if a suspicion could have been raised against
the validity of the marriage itself.   Defective as
Lady Jane's title to the crown certainly was, it does
not appear that either of Lord Orford's objections
to her claim have the least validity, with the exception of the latter part of the first; and although
that must strike us at the present day as being
unanswerable, it is suggested that the circumstances which have been detailed, might have divested it of great part of its weight in the eyes of
such of her contemporaries as were disposed to
support her claim to the imperial dignity.

The fate of Lady Jane Grey's immediate kindred may be related in a few words.   Her father,
the Duke of Suffolk, underwent the execution of

his sentence on Tower Hill, on the 23rd February,
1554, eleven days after his daughter and son-in-
law fell victims to his ambition: he is stated to
have confessed the justice of his punishment, and
to have suffered with fortitude and resignation.
His widow married, secondly, Adrian Stokes, Esq.
a gentleman who held a situation in her household, but by him she had no issue, and died in
1559. A warrant was issued by Queen Elizabeth
to the Kings of Arms, to cause the royal ensigns,
with a proper distinction, to be borne at her funeral, and placed on her monument, from respect to
her kindred to her majesty.ᵃ The only children
of the Duke and Duchess of Suffolk that survived,

ᵃ The following is a literal copy of the warrant alluded
to, and which is introduced from its being of some interest,
and because it proves that the Duchess died about the end
of October, 1559, whilst Mr. Howard and most other writers
assert that her decease occurred in 1563.

BY THE QUENE,

Trusty and welbeloved we great you well,
letting you to understand, that for the good zeale, and affection wiche we of long tyme have borne to our dearly beloved cousyn the Lady Fraunces late Duches of Suff', and
specially for that she is lynyally descended from our grandfather King Henry the Sevinthe; as also for other causes
and consyderations as thereunto moving in perpetuall
memory of the same, we have thought it requisyte and ex-
pedyent to gruunte and give unto her and to her posteryte

besides Lady Jane Grey, were two other daughters, Katherine and Mary. Lady Katherine was

an augmentation of our armes to be borne with the difference
to the same by us assigned, and the same to beare in the
place of the first quarter, and so to be placyd with the arms
of her auncestors as by the orders of our office it is manifest,
according to the Skochin, by us directed unto you in that
behaulf, that is to saye, our armes withe a bordure gouboney
golde and azur wich shal be an apparent declaration of here
consanguynyte unto us. Whereupon we will and requier
you to see the same entyrd into your registers and recordes;
and at this her funerall to plasse the same augmentation
withe her auncesters armes, in banners, baneroles, lozenges,
and scochins, as otherwisse, when it shall be thought mete
and convenyent. And theis our Letters shalbe your suffy-
cyent warant and discharge in this behaulf. Geeven under
our signett at our Palleis of Westmaster, the thierde daye of
December, in y* seconde Yeare of our Reigne.

To our trusty and welbeloved Servant, Sr. Gilbert Dethicke, Knight, alias
Garter our Princypall King of Armes,
and William Harvy, Esquier, aliasClaren-
cieuix, Kinge of Armes of the Southe
parte of this our Realme of England,
and to either of them.

MS. in the College of Arms, marked
I. 9 f. 153.ᵇ and printed in *Sandford's
Genealogical History*, p. 537.

The inscription on the Duchess of Suffolk's tomb in
Westminster Abbey, of which a copy is subjoined, does not
contain the date of her death.

first married, or rather perhaps betrothed to
Henry Herbert, son and heir apparent of William,
Earl of Pembroke, but that union does not appear
to have been consummated;[a] and she afterwards
became the wife of Edward Seymour, Earl of
Hertford, son of the Protector. The circumstances
attending this alliance, and the misfortunes which
from the jealously of Queen Elizabeth, it entailed

Here lyeth the Ladie Frances, Dutchess of Southfolke,
daughter to Charles Brandon, Duke of Southfolke, and
Mary the French Queene, first wife to Henrie, Duke of
Southfolke, and after to Adrian Stock, Esquire.

In clariss. Dom. Franciscæ Suf-
folciæ quondam Ducissæ.
Epicedion.
Nil Decus aut splendor, nil regia nomina prosunt.
Splendida divitis, nil juvat ampla Domus.
Omnia fluxerunt, Virtutis sola remansit.
Gloria, Tartareis, non abolenda rogis.
Nupta duci prius est, uxor post Armigeri Stok.
Funere nunc valeas, consociata Deo.

[a] Fuller attributes the non-completion of this marriage
to political motives, for he observes of Lady Katherine Grey,
"She was born at Bradgate, and (when her father was in
height) married to Henry Lord Herbert, son and heir to the
Earl of Pembroke; but the politic old Earl perceiving the
case altered, and what was the high way to honour, turned
into the ready road to ruin, got pardon from Queen Mary,
and broke the marriage quite off."

on the Earl and herself, are too well known to require repetition. From this marriage some of the most illustrious families in the kingdom are descended; but the entire representation of the elder line of the once powerful house of Grey of Groby, and consequently of Lady Jane Grey, is now vested in the Duchess of Buckingham and Chandos.

Katherine, Countess of Hertford, died on the 26 January, 1567, after having been for nine years a state prisoner: it appears from the statement of an intelligent writer in the Gentleman's Magazine,[a] that she did not, as Fuller relates, die in the Tower; for although Mr. Bayley[b] informs us that on the 5th September, 4 Eliz. 1562, "The Ladie Katherine Grey and the Erle of Hartford" were prisoners there, yet from the following extract from Reyce's MSS. relating to Suffolk Antiquities, now in the College of Arms, and cited by the anonymous writer just mentioned, it may be inferred that she was subsequently confined at Yoxford, in Suffolk, and where it is certain she was buried.

"There be buried in the church and chancel at Yoxford, the bowels of ye Lady Katherine, wife of Edward Seimour, Earl of Hartford. She was

---

[a] Vol. XCIII. Part ii. p. 11.

[b] *History of the Tower.*

daughter of Henry Grey, Duke of Suffolk, and of Mary, the French Queen, the younger of the two daughters of King Henry VIII :—of the elder, K. James and K. Charles were descended. This Lady Katherine had been committed prisoner to Sir. Owen Hopton, Lieftenant of the Tower, for marrying without the Queen's knowledge, and was by ·him kept at Cockfield Hall, in Yoxfield, being his house, where she died. I have been told by aged people in Yoxford, that after her death, a little dog she had would never more eat any meat, but lay and died upon her grave."

The preceding statement; though not strictly correct in the description of the Countess's connection with the blood royal, is doubtlessly in other respects authentic, as it is corroborated by the following entry in the Parish Register at Yoxford.

"The Lady Katherine Grey, buried 21st Feb. 1567."

Her death is said to have taken place on the 26 January, 1567, but it is singular if she died on that day that she should not have been buried until nearly a month afterwards.

Lady Mary Grey, the Duke of Suffolk's youngest daughter, was deformed in her person;[a] and Fuller, with his peculiar quaintness, remarks, that "frighted with the infelicity of her two

---

[a] *Baker's Chronicle, Ed.* 1657, p. 309.

sisters, she forgot her honor to remember her safely, and married one whom she could love, and none need fear, Martin Keyes, of Kent, Esq. who was a Judge at Court, but only of doubtful cast of dice, being Serjeant Porter." She died without issue, on the 20th of April, 1578.

To the memoir of the life of Lady Jane Grey, it is almost unnecessary to add any general delineation of her character, for the actions of mankind, if related with fidelity, are far more satisfactory evidence of merit than any deduction from them by the biographer. In the instance of this exemplary woman, no other language than that of unqualified praise can possibly be used: her conduct as a daughter and a wife afford ample scope for panegyric; and her extraordinary attainments, fortitude, and piety, have ever been the subject of admiration. In the assumption of the royal dignity —the only action of her life which can be at all censured—we have seen that she yielded to the commands of her parents and the entreaties of her husband, rather than to any ambitious feelings of her own; and it appears extremely probable, that the most powerful motive which induced her to forget her allegiance to her sovereign, was the certainty that no other means existed by which the lives and fortunes of her nearest relatives could have been preserved. Thus, her every action seems to have

originated in virtue; and although neither her
beauty, her acquirements, nor her innocence, could
save her from a premature and disgraceful death,
it may with truth be affirmed, that on the tomb of
LADY JANE GREY, perhaps with more justice than
on that of any other inheritor of mortality, might
the emphatic lines of our bard be inscribed,

> "Now boast thee death! in thy possession lies
> A lass unparalled."

Since the publication of this Volume, the Editor was accidently informed that two documents of considerable interest connected with Lady Jane Grey were preserved in the library of New College, Oxford; and he gratefully acknowledges the kindness of its highly respectable librarian, John Shute Duncan, Esq. senior Fellow of New College, in acquainting him with their existence, and for permitting him to transcribe them for this work. They are contained in the book of original warrants addressed to the keeper of the Palace of Westminster by Edward VI., by Lady Jane Grey whilst she usurped the royal dignity, and by Queen Mary, for the delivery of silks, velvet, jewelry, clocks, the will of Henry VII., deeds and other writings, &c. Many of these warrants, which it is presumed are not generally known, are highly curious, and afford minute information about wearing apparel, jewelry, clocks, dials, &c. of the period. The articles ordered to be delivered were often presents to a royal favorite, and sometimes consisted of silk or velvet for their wedding clothes. During the reign of Mary numerous warrants occur for silk and velvet for copes and vestments for the service of the altar, indicative of the restoration of the ancient religion; some of which were given to the Friars of Greenwich, and the rest to religious houses in London. One of the warrants issued by her is peculiar, as it orders the keeper of the Palace to give up to the person named, certain pictures of our Lord, of Saints, &c. then, it would appear from the words of the instrument, laid aside as lumber, part for the purpose of being bestowed on the churches specified, and the remainder to parish churches. Another peculiarity in these warrants, illustrative of the manners of the times, consists in the minuteness with which each article is described, and the importance which was evidently attached to them by the signature and signet of the Sovereign, and in some cases of the whole of the Privy Council also, being necessary to authorize the delivery of some yards of paltry silk, or of a few trifling jewels! Many of these documents would have been given at length, but the Editor did not feel justified in drawing more largely on that kindness to which he is indebted for the two relating to Lady Jane Grey. They will, however, he hopes, be introduced to the public under infinitely better auspices; for if the numerous duties of Mr. Duncan permit, it is probable that that accomplished gentleman may be induced to undertake their publication.

So few of the documents signed by Lady Jane Grey whilst she exercised the royal functions, are extant, that the following are of sufficient importance to demand the exertion which has been made, by printing some extra pages immediately after the Editor had transcribed them, to give them a place in this volume. It will be seen that the first was signed on the day of her accession, and the velvet was evidently wanted to cover her temporary throne and its appendages. From the second, dated four days afterwards, we learn that the jewels which formed the personal ornaments of the Sovereign, had been previously delivered into Lady Jane's own hands, pursuant to her verbal commands. But perhaps the most curious fact connected with these documents, besides the rigid and tradesman-like attention with which, from the marginal notes, it is manifest, each article was compared with the list, is, that the words "THE QUENE" have been lined over with a pen, from which we may infer that no public instrument of the unhappy Jane's bearing the title that produced her destruction was permitted to remain in its original state among the public Archives. The warrants themselves could not be destroyed, as they accounted for the expenditure and transfer of certain parts of the Crown property; but the loyalty of Mary's servant's was *of course* too fervent, and their attachment to their Sovereign too jealous, to allow so hated an appellation to remain attached to her rival's name, even though the tomb covered that rival's mutilated remains!

In Harl. MSS. 611, f. 1, is a warrant addressed to the Marquess of Winchester, the Lord Treasurer, by Mary, dated 20th September, 1553, stating, that upon the delivery of "jewels and stuff" by the Lady Jane Grey the 20th of July last, which she had received of him the 12th of the same month, it appeared that the parcels mentioned were wanting; but that as her Majesty understood by the Marquess's diligence all the rest which had been given to her were recovered, though, "being at the same time in danger," she hopes, by using similar exertions, the articles in question will also be found. This list, though extremely curious, does not appear to contain any of the jewels and trinkets enumerated in the following warrant. Mr. Howard, however, in a note to his "*Lady Jane Grey and her Times,*" p. 257, alludes to jewels &c. delivered by command of Lady Jane on the 14th of July, and gives a list of a few of them "to mark the manners of the times," which he states to have been taken from the original order; but, as is unfortunately too frequently the case in that amusing publication, he omits to state where the document which he cites is preserved. As the few extracts there given agree with the catalogue in the warrant to Sir Andrew Dudley, that instrument is probably the one referred to.

By another Warrant from Queen Mary to the Marquess of Winchester, likewise preserved in Harl. MSS. 611, dated 20th August, 1553, acknowledging the receipt " of all these percells of mony, jewells, golde, stone, perle, and other stuffe hereafter mentioned and expressed in sixteen leaves of paper written on both sides," an interesting account is exhibited of the Crown jewels of the period; among which, or, among the list of the "Percell of the Duchess of Somerset's stuff in the chardge of Sir Andrew Dudley, Knight," in f. 10 of the same Manuscript, many, if not all, of those delivered on the 14th July to Lady Jane Grey are enumerated.

The Manuscript in the Harleian collection, just quoted, contains likewise an account of coin received from Lady Jane Grey, on Wednesday, 26th July, 1553, and also from Lord Guildford Dudley.

JANE, ~~THE QUENE~~.

BY THE QUENE.

WE woll and commande you that immea-diatlie uppon the sight herof ye delyver or cause to be delyvered for oure use of oure silke and other stuffe remayning in yor custody and charge, these parcells following, videl't, twentie yards of crymesen velvet to cover two chayres and two close stooles, and also one pece of fyne holland clothe contayning a xxv ells. And one pece of courser holland clothe contayning a xxx^{ti} ells iij quartes. And these our l'res signed wth oure hand shalbe yor sufficient warrannt and discharge in this behalf. Yeaven under oure signet at the Towre the xth daye of Julye in the first yere of our Reign.[b]

To oure trustie and welbeloved uncle,

[a] Sic in the original.
[b] In the margin of the original are the figures.

\ ·94
\ ·96 \ ·95

Sr Andrewe Duddeley,[a] Knight of
thordre and keper of our palaice of
Westm^r.

Indorsed,

Warrannt for the delyvre of xx^{ti} yards of crymsene
velvet and ij peces of holland clothe for the quene's grace.

[a] A slight account of this personage is given in a note
to p. cv of the Memoir of Lady Jane Grey, but nothing is
stated by his biographers on the subject of his marriage.
Among the Warrants preserved in the volume in the
library of New College, Oxford, before noticed, is one addressed to Sir Andrew Dudley, dated 8th June, 7 Edw. VI.
1553, authorizing him to deliver silk for apparel for himself
and Lady Margaret Clifford, daughter of the Earl of Cumberland, "for both your weddings;" from which it would
appear that the Duke of Northumberland's plan of aggran-
dizing his family by alliances with the blood royal, extended
to marrying his brother to Lady Margaret Clifford, who was
the only child of the Earl of Cumberland, by Eleanor Brandon, niece of King Henry the eighth; on whom, as is
stated in a former page, by that monarch's will, failing the
issue of Lady Jane Grey's mother, the Crown was entailed.
Her union with Sir Andrew never, however, took place,
for about two years afterwards, on the 7th February, 1555,
she married the Earl of Derby.

JANE, ~~THE QUENE~~.[a]

A note of certaine Jewells and other thinges delyvered unto the Quenes hyghness by   Sturton,[b] Esquier, the xiiij day of July, 1553, in the fyerst yere of her hyghnes reigne.

1 First one tablet vj square with ij faces and vj perles.

[a] Sic in the original.

[b] Evidently Arthur Stourton, who, during the reign of Mary, held the office of Keeper of the Palace of Westminster. He was the third son of William, 6th Lord Stourton, by Elizabeth, daughter of Edmund Dudley, and half sister of John, Duke of Northumberland. In the collection of original warrants to the Keepers of the Palace of Westminster, in the library of New College, is an original letter without date or superscription, of which the following is a literal copy. It was undoubtedly addressed to Arthur Stourton, just mentioned, who, it may be conjectured from its contents, held some office under his uncle, Sir Andrew Dudley, in the Royal Household before he succeeded him in the situation of Keeper of the Palace of Westminster.

Nevieu I must nede have three yards q^r more of the purple velvet, and as moche of the Chrimsen velvet otherwys the garment wyl be spylt

Y^r loving Unckell

NORTHUMBERLAND.

2 Itm one broche with a woman comyng out of a cloude with children.

3 Itm one other broche of golde with a story in it having xix table rubies and ij table dyamandes and viij rede rubies above it.

4 Itm two pece with rubies and iij pece with dyamands and iij other pecies with ij perles in a pece, all serving for byllymentes.

5 Itm one other pece with a dyamant for a girdle. Item one other broche of the storie of a sacrifing having on it ij red rubies and v little diamandes and a faire emerall.

6 Itm a fishe of gold being a toothe pyk.

7 Itm a litle pendant having one great perle and vi lytle perles at it.

8 Itm, one tablet of the picture of a woman graven in a stone like a jacent, with a faire pearle pendent.

9 Itm one tablet of agathe garnishing with golde with a diall in it with a ruby, and a dyamand garnished with smalle stones having a perle pendannt.

10 Itm another broche of agathe wth St Jones heade, garnished with golde.

11 Itm one dewbery of golde.

12 Itm a faire tablet wth Cupids face graven in stone wth a triangle diamande set in it.

13 Itm a tablet, boke fashion, w^h story of St David on the one side, and on thother side iiij blew saphires.

14 Itm a colet wth v perles and a counterset stone.

15 Itm a flowre wth white Saphier and iij perles pendant.

16 Itm a broche wth a woman of mother of perle and a saile over her head.

17 Itm a newte of silver white.

18 Itm a tablet wth a white saphier, and a blew, and ballesse, and a perle pendant.

19 Itm a tablet of cristall and jacinde with a picture wthin them.

20 Itm a tablet of agathe wth Saint Katerin wthin it.

21 Itm a floure wth blew saphier square, and a amatist square.

22 Itm the l're ℜ with a great balez and iij perles pendent.

23 Itm a floure of golde of iij crosses and a floure de luse of diamandes, and a perle pendannt.

24 Itm a pece of golde wth a rede rubie in it for a girdle.

24 Itm a broche with an agathe engraven wth a story, enamelled black and white.

25 Itm a tablet of golde enamelled black and white with a clock in it.

26 Itm a booke garnished wth gold and covered wth black velvet.

27 Itm a broche of gold wth a face in agathe.

28 Itm two clasbes, one with a floure de luce of dyamandes, and th'other with a blew saphiere.

29 Itm a tablet of golde iij square enamelled blacke.

30 Itm one other paire of clasbes one wth an agathe, and thother enamelled blacke.

31 Itm a broche of golde enamelled black wth a face agathe.

33^a Itm another broche wth a woman holding a floure de luce of diamandes in her hande.

34 Itm a floure of golde wth a great ballesse and vi perles.

35 Itm a broche of gold, wth a story in blew w^{th}in a christall.

36 Itm a broche of golde with the picture of our Lady of agathe, broken.

37 Itm a broche of a George of mother of perle.

38 Itm a crosse of ten dyamandes and iij perles pendant.

39 Itm two clasbes, one like a scalope shell, thother with a floure of rubies.

* No. 32 is omitted.

40 Itm a broche of an agathe with a horse in it.

41 Itm a tablet of golde hanged by a chaine with
a Saint Jones heade and viij stoth pearles.

42 Itm a George of golde the ground enamelled
blewe.

43 Itm a hole George of golde set with diamandes with a rubie in the Dragon.

44 Itm a floure wth iij rede rubies and v pearles.

45 Itm a cipher wth a floure de luce and a crowne
set wth diamandes and iij perles pendannt.

46 Itm a tablet of golde, on thone side the Salu-
tation of our Lady, and thother side the Re-
surrection.

47 Itm a crosse of golde of the picture of Christ,
enamelled white and red.

48 Itm a broche of golde wth a picture of a man
in blewe stone.

49 Itm a small tablet of golde wth an Antyr
heade of agathe and a perle hanging at it.

50 Itm a small tablet of a cornelian wth pictures
enamelled white.

51 Itm a tablet of a picture of our Lady of Pitt'
in a blewe stone.

52 Itm an Egle enamelled white garnished with
vij counterfet pearles and a counterfet saphier.

53 Itm a booke garnished wth acornes of golde.

54 Itm one girdle cont' xxxviij pecies wth a pendaunt having at it sondry small chaynes, the
girdle enamelled black.

55 Itm another girdle cont' xxxv peces of goldesmiths work enamelled red, with a pendant
without tassell.

56 Itm another girdle cont' lxxij pecies of goldesmythes work enamelled white and blacke,
with a rounde knobb or pendant at it.

57 Itm another girdle cont' lij peceis of golde-
smyths work enamelled black and white.

58 Itm a flagon chayne of golde cont' xlvj lyncks,
iij qr'ts of a yarde in length.

59 Itm a paire of beads of white purstayen, with
viij gawdes of golde and xxxviij beads of
white, with a tassell of golde and silke.

60 Itm one paire of beades of lapis Lazarus cont'
xlvj stones viij gawdes and small pecies of
golde betwene the stones, and a tassell of
golde.

61 Itm another paire of beades of the same
perele fashion, cont' xlij stones viij gawdes of
golde, and betwene every of them a litle beade
of golde.

62 Itm a paire of beads of rede currall cont' xlviij
stones viii gawdes set wth small garnetts and
betweene every stone a litle pece of golde.

63 Itm a paire of beades of jarnick cont' xxxvj
stones viij gawdes, between every stone a
lytle pece of golde having a knope with a
tasell of smale chaynes of golde, lacking one.

64 Itm a paire of beades of jeate cont' xlij stones
vij gawdes and a knoppe, enamelled black,
wth small chaines and litle peceies of golde
betwene ev'y stone.

65 Itm a paire of beades of currall, acorne fashion,
cont' xlviij stones and vij gawdes enamelled
black wth small bead stones between them,
having a tassell silke and golde.

66 Itm a paire of beades of golde cont' xlvi peces
of goldesmythes worke enamelled white and
black with vi gawdes like ostretche fethers
wth litle peces betweene, to the numb'r of L
and a tassell of golde and silver.

67 Itm a paire of beades of jacinke cont' lx
stones wth viii gawdes of golde, and betwene
every stone a litle beade of golde and a tassell

68 Itm a paire of beades of agathes cont' xiiij
stones small and great, wth viij gawdes of gold,
wth perles and a tassell of Venise golde.

69 Itm a paire of beades of golde, cont' lxvi beades
and viii gawdes and a tassell of Venise golde.

70 Itm a paire of beads, cont' lxiiij stones of
Ibony wth lxiiij pec' of golde between the
stones, wth a tassell of blacke silke.

71 Itm a girdle of gold like fryers knots, cont'
xliij pec' wth a knoppe of golde wth small
chaines and bells at it.

72 Itm a paire of beades of blew stones garnished

wth gold, flagon fashion, cont' xlviij stones
wth vi gawdes of golde enamelled black wth a
knoppe of chaynes of gold and silver.

73 Itm a paire of beades like turkesis cont' lx
blewe stones.

74 Itm a paire of beades cont' lviij beads of golde
crymery worke, wth vi gawdes of the same
worke and a small tassell.

75 Itm a paire of beades of gold cont' xii small
beades of crymery work.

76 Itm a chaine of golde cont' xxiiij lyncks
wrethed and playne.

77 Itm iij smale chaynes of golde, every of them
one aglet to spare. being half a yarde long, laking almost
one naile.

78 Itm lxviij faire paire of aglets of golde and
ii paire to spare. one od aglet, enamelled white and black.

79 Itm xviij paire of aglets of golde enamelled
one aglet to spare. russett.

80 Itm xix paire of aglets of golde wth crosses,
enamelled black and white, and one od aglet.

80 Itm xiiij paire of small aglets of golde, enamelled black.

81 Itm xxxvij paire of aglets of golde of sondry
sorts gret and small and one broken peee of
an aglett.

.. Itm **xxviij** aglets of golde, acorne fashion, enamelled black.

82 Itm **xij** bead stones of golde upon a white
  threade.

83 Itm **xxiiij** od peces of goldesmythes worke of
  sondry sorts for billyments, enamelled black.

84 Itm **x** peces of goldesmithes work for a girdle,
  enamelled black, with a pendaunt like a piller
  belonging to the same.

85 Itm **xvi** peces of goldesmithes worke for bil-
  lements, enamelled white and blewe.

86 Itm **xv** buttons of golde of crymery work,
  enamelled black and white, sondry sorteis.

87 Itm **ij** purses hangers of silver and gilt.

.. Itm **v** small buttons set wth table rubies.

88 Itm two peces for a billement of goldesmithes
  work, with foure perles in a pece, and a rose
  in the mi'dle.

90 Itm a carcanett wth **xv** dyamands set in golde,
  and between of every of them four small
  peces of gold and perles.

92 Itm a carcanett wth **xx** rubies sett in golde,
  wth **xxxv** pearles in bondells of gold enamelled
  black with a floure at the same set wth **iij**
  table rubies and a rede rubye wth a perle pendannt.

93 Itm another carcanett wth **ix** table diamands
  set in golde and **lxxxv** pearles and other

small perles to the nombre of xx wth a floure
of goldẽ and iiij table diamands and iij perles
pendannt.

94 Itm xxi pearles, small and great on a thread.

95 Itm a carcanett of golde, fetterlock fashion,
enamelled black, in some places broken, cont'
xliij peces and xlvj pearles.

96 Itm a carcanett cont' xxxviij great perles.

97 Itm another carcanett cont' xxv knots of perles
in every knott iiij perles, and between them
xxxvj xix'es* of gold.

98 Itm a faire floure of golde enamelled white and
black, set in it a emerall, and a ruby and a
perle pendant.

97 Itm xviij perles small and great and vij small
xix'es* of gold together in a paper.

99 Itm a paire of brasselets of xx^{ti} blew and
iii perles and one   rede stones and ij jacincks.
pipe to spare.

100 Itm a paire of braseletts of xiiij peces
of gold, enamelled black and white, wth rubies
and diamands set in them.

101 Itm another paire of brasselets of gold of
xxij peces, enamelled black and rede.

102 Itm a paire of brasseletts of flagon chayne
wth jacincks.

* Query.

103 Itm lxxvj buttones of golde crymery woke, in every button vi perles.

104 Itm five other buttons of a bygger sorte, enamelled black, wth vi perles in every button.

105 Itm a George of gold wthin a garter, hanging at a black lace.

106 Itm xi peces of goldesmithes worke for a billament, enamelled white and rede.

107 Itm xxx^{ti} small turkeses, litle worthe.

108 Itm viii table diamands set in colletts of golde.

109 Itm a spone of golde wth a saphier in the knoppe.

110 Itm an olde garter with the buckill pendannt, and l'res of golde, enamelled black.

111 Itm a touchestone set in golde.

112 Itm vi rounde buttones, enamelled rede, set in very of them five counterfeit stones.

113 Itm a pece of a brasselet cont' vij pec', with counterfet stones, and ij peces with ostreche fathers.

114 Itm five rings of golde, iij of them rubies, one amatist, and the other an agathe.

115 Itm certen small garnetts in a paper.

116 Itm one abillyment of goldesmithes worke, cont' xij rubies set in gold and xxij pec', set wth ij perles in a pec'e.

117 Itm another a billyment wth xij table diamondes set in golde and xiij peces of goldesmithes worke with ij perles in a pece.

* t

118 Itm another abilliment with xvi rede rubies
set in golde and xvij peces of goldesmithes
worke wth ij perles in a pece.

119 Itm another abillyment wth xvi peces of
goldesmithes worke wth vi perles in a pece,
and xv peces of goldesmithes werke between
them, enamelled black.

120 Itm another billement cont' xxv peces of
goldesmiths work, enamelled black.

121 Itm another abillment cont' xxv peces of goldesmiths worke ruff fashions, enamelled black.

122 Itm another abillment cont' xxx peces of
goldesmiths work, enamelled white.

123 Itm another abillment cont' xl peces of
goldesmithes worke, boll fashione, enamelled
black and white.

124 Itm another abillment cont' xx long peces of
goldesmithes work, enamelled black and white.

125 Itm xlix paire of greate agletes of golde
one button   crymery work.
to spare.

126 Itm xx triangle buttons of gold, enamelled
black.

127 Itm xlviij damaskin buttons.

128 Itm a coller of St Michell cont' xliiij knotts
and xlvij skalopp shell, and a Michell hanging at it.

129 Itm two glasses wth ostreche fethers thr'on,

set in gold, garnished wth sondry smale stones
and an Antik face, the handle being cristall;
and thother of silver garnished wth five rede
rubies set in golde, the handle christall.

130 Itm a clock of damasked worke, booke fashion.

131 Itm a chest of silver, wicker fashion, with a
litle pot and a bowl of golde wth a . . . . in it.

132 Itm a litle square boxe covered with purple
velvet garnished with copper gilt, having in it
ten diamonds set in ringe, whereof iij be of
faire table diamonds, iij pointed diamonds, the
rest of a smale sorte

one but a   ⌐Itm four rubies, two of ye iiij, faire
garnet.   tables set in ringe.

    Itm iij turkesis set in ringe and two
    table emeraldes set in ringe.

133   Itm ij ringes like serpents, one wth a
    diamand and thother with a perle.

    Itm a litle ring wth iij diamonds and
    foure small rubyes. ' Itm ij litle
    ringes, thone wth a birde; and
    ⌐thother wth a hart enamelled rede.

Trustie and welbeloved, we grete you
well, and where ye have by o^r order
and com'ndment, given unto you by
worde of mouthe, delivered unto o^r
owne handes, Jewells and other

thinges before mentioned ; we mind-
ing you discharged in this behalf, and
that y^r conformitie in the delivery
of the said Jewells wthout warrant
shall not be any waies p'udicial unto
y^o, do by these p's'nts acknowledge
the recept of the said Jewells and
other things before written. And
do hereby acquite and discharge you
of the same, for which purpose these
shalbe y^r sufficient warraunt. Yeaven at o^r Towre of London the
xiiijth of July in the firste yere of
o^r reigne.

  [a] To oure trustie and welbeloved uncle S^r
Andrewe Dudley, Knight of the order.

  [a] Written in a different ink and with another pen, but
apparently in the same hand. Over each of the above articles the letters *ex* are written, as if to mark that every item
had been compared with the catalogue.

NOTES.

The frequent reference which has been made in the preceding memoir to the statutes passed in the reign of Henry the Eighth, relative to the succession, as well as to the will of that monarch, makes it desirable that a full abstract of them should be appended thereto. The proof which these acts afford of the contemptible venality of the Parliaments of the period; the extraordinary dereliction of all moral principle which they exhibit, not only in perverting justice and humanity to gratify the caprice of a tyrant, but also the shameless hypocrisy of attempting to cover their own baseness by the pretence of acting acceptably to the Almighty, and in accordance to his laws; and still more, the importance of these documents as data for the impartial consideration of the question of Lady Jane's pretensions to the throne, render them highly curious; and it is hoped, justifies the introduction of so long a note.

The first Statute connected with the succession was that of 25th Henry VIII. cap. 22, passed in the early part of the year 1534, to confirm his divorce from Katherine of Arragon, and to legalize his marriage with Anne Boleyn.

The Preamble recites "that since it is the natural inclination of every man gladly and willingly to provide for the surety of both his title and succession, although it touch his only private cause," they, the Lords Spiritual and Temporal, and the Commons in the present Parliament assembled, reckon themselves bounden to beseech and instant

his Highness, although they doubt not his princely heart
and wisdom, to forsee and provide for the perfect surety
of both him and his most lawful succession and heirs, upon
which depended all their joy and wealth; in whom also was
united, and knit the only mere true inheritance and title of
this realm, without any contradiction. Wherefore they,
calling to mind the great divisions which in times past had
been in this realm, by reason of several titles pretended to
the Imperial Crown, &c. "in consideration whereof your
said most humble and obedient subjects, the Nobles and
Commons of this realm, calling further to their remembrance
that the good unity, peace, and wealth of this realm, and the
succession of the subjects of the same most especially and
principally above all worldly things, consisteth and resteth
in the certainty and surety of the procreation and posterity
of your Highness, in whose most royal person at this present
time is no manner of doubt nor question, do therefore most
humbly beseech your Highness that it may please your Majesty, that it may be enacted by your Highness with the
assent of the Lords Spiritual and Temporal, and the Commons
in this Parliament assembled, and by the authority of the
same, that the marriage heretofore solemnized between your
Highness and the Lady Katherine, being before lawful wife
to Prince Arthur your elder brother, which by him was car-
nally known, as doth duly appear by sufficient prove as a
lawful process had and made before Thomas, by the suffer-
ance of God, now Archbishop of Canterbury, and Metropolitan and Primate of all this realm, shall be by authority of
this present Parliament, definitively, clearly, and absolutely
declared, deemed, and adjuged to be against the laws of
Almighty God, and also accepted and reputed, and taken of
no value nor effect, but utterly void and adnychyled, and

the separation thereof made by the said Archbishop, shall be good and effectual to all intents and purposes, any license, dispensation, or any other act or acts going afore or ensuing the same, to the contrary thereof in any wise notwithstanding. And that every such license, dispensation, act or acts, thing or things, heretofore had, made, done, or to be done to the contrary, shall be void and of none effect; and that the said Lady Katherine shall be from henceforth called and reputed only Dowager to Prince Arthur, and not Queen of this realm. And that the lawful matrimony had and solemnized between your Highness and your most dear and entirely beloved wife Queen Anne, shall be established and taken for undoubtful, true, sincere, and perfect, ever hereafter, according to the just judgment of Thomas, Archbishop of Canterbury, Metropolitan and Primate of all this realm, whose grounds of judgment have been confirmed as well by the Holy Clergy of this realm in both the convocations, and by both the universities thereof, as by the universities of Bonony, Padua, Paris, Orleans, Toulouse, Anjou, and divers others, and also by the private writing of many right excellent and learned men, which grounds so confirmed and judgment of the said Archbishop ensuing the same, together with your marriage solemnized between your Highness and your said lawful wife Queen Anne, we your said subjects, both Spiritual and Temporal, do purely, plainly, constantly, and firmly accept, approve, and ratify for good and consonant to the laws of Almighty God without error or default, most humbly beseeching your Majesty that it may be so established for ever by your most gracious and royal assent." The Act then enumerates the different prohibited degrees of marriage, and states that none can dispense with God's law; and it is enacted that no one of what degree, estate, or dig-

nity soever, shall in future marry within the prohibited degrees; that if any have before been married within the said
degrees of kindred, such marriage shall be dissolved and
the issue of the same "shall not be lawful nor legitimate;"
and that persons so married shall be separated by the sentence of the ordinary only, without any appeal to Rome. It
then proceeds, "And also be it enacted by authority aforesaid, that all the issue had and procreate, or hereafter to be
had and procreate between your Highness and your said
most dear and entirely beloved wife Queen Anne, shall be
your lawful children and be inheritable, and inherit according to the course of inheritance and laws of this realm, the
Imperial Crown of the same with all dignities, honors, pre-
eminencies, prerogatives, authorities, and jurisdictions to
the same annexed or belonging, in as large and ample
manner as your Highness to this present time hath the same
as King of this realm, the inheritance thereof to be and remain to your said children and right heirs in manner and
form as hereafter shall be declared. That is to say, first,
the said Imperial Crown and other the premises shall be to
your Majesty and to your heirs of your body lawfully begotten; that is to say, to the first son of your body between
your Highness and your said lawful wife Queen Anne begotten, and to the heirs of the body of the same first son
lawfully begotten; and for default of such heirs then to the
second son of your body and of the body of the said Queen
Anne begotten, and to the heirs of the body of the said
second son lawfully begotten; and so to every son of your
body and of the body of the said Queen Anne begotten, and
to the heirs of the body of every such son begotten according to the course of inheritance in that behalf. And if it
shall happen your said dear and entirely beloved wife Queen

Anne, to decease without issue male of the body of your Highness to be gotten, (which God defend) then the same Imperial Crown and all other the premises to be to your Majesty as is aforesaid, and to the son and heir male of your body lawfully begotten, and to the heirs of the body of the same son and heir male lawfully begotten. And for default of such issue then to your second son of your body lawfully begotten, and to the heirs of the body of the same second son lawfully begotten; and so from son and heir male to son and heir male, and to the heirs of the several bodies of every such son and heir male to be gotten according to the course of inheritance in like manner and form as is above said. And for default of such sons of your body begotten and of the heirs of the several bodies of every such sons lawfully begotten, that then the said Imperial Crown and other the premises shall be to the issue female between your Majesty and your said most dear and entirely beloved wife Queen Anne begotten: that is to say, first to the eldest issue female which is the Lady Elizabeth, now Princess, and to the heirs of her body lawfully begotten; and for default of such issue, then to the second issue female and to the heirs of her body lawfully begotten, and so from issue female to issue female, and to their heirs of their bodies one after another by course of inheritance, according to their ages, as the Crown of England hath been accustomed and ought to go in cases where there be heirs females to the same. And for default of such issue, then the said Imperial Crown and all other the premises shall be in the right heirs of your Highness for ever." It is then provided, that if any person shall maliciously do any thing by writing, print, deed, or act, to the peril of the King, or to the prejudice of his marriage with Queen Anne, or of the issue inheritable to

the Crown under this act, he shall be declared guilty of High
Treason, and that those committing such offences by word
only shall be declared guilty of misprision of Treason. The
eighth clause enacts, that upon the King's demise, the issue
male under eighteen years of age, or female issue unmarried
under sixteen, who should inherit the Crown, should be
under the guardianship of their mother, "with such other
counsellors of your realm as your Majesty in your life time
shall depute and assign by your will or otherwise;" and
that if any person by writing or exterior deed, or act, procure or do, or cause to be procured or done any thing or
things to the let or disturbance of the same, that then such
opposers shall be subject to the penalties of High Treason.
The ninth clause provides, that all subjects shall be sworn to
the performance of this act on pain of misprision of Treason;
and the tenth and concluding clause enacts, that the pro-
hibition of marriages within the degrees mentioned in this
act, "shall always be taken and interpreted, and expounded
of such marriages, where marriages were solemnized, and
carnal knowledge had."

Queen Anne Boleyn was executed on Friday, the 19th
May, 28 Hen. VIII. 1536, and by Statute 28 Hen. VIII.
cap. 7. passed in June or July, 1536, of which the following is an abstract, her marriage with the King was declared
void *ab initio*, and the issue of it, namely the Princess afterwards Queen Elizabeth illegitimated. It is remarkable,
that although the crimes of adultery and incest, which
formed the *pretence* for Anne Boleyn's disgrace and murder,
are alluded to in this act, still she is not expressly charged
with either; the words being merely that she *confederated*
with her brother Lord Rochfort, Norris, Weston, and Sme-

ton, and "committed most detestable and abominable treasons."

The Preamble, after reciting the Statute 25 Hen. VIII.
cap. 22. just noticed, for limiting the succession, proceeds :
"And albeit most dread Sovereign Lord, that the said Acts
were then made, as it was then thought by your Majesty, Nobles, and Commons, upon a pure, perfect, and clear foundation, thinking the said marriage then had between your Highness and the said Lady Anne, in their consciences to have
been pure, sincere, perfect and good, and so was reputed,
accepted, and taken in the Realm, 'till now of late that
God of his infinite goodness, from whom no secret things
can be hid, hath caused to be brought to light evident and
open knowledge as well of certain just, true, and lawful
impediment unknown at the making of the said acts, and
since that time confessed by the said Lady Anne, before the
most Reverend Father in God, Thomas, Archbishop of Canterbury, Metropolitan and Primate of all England, sitting
judicially for the same, by the which plainly appeareth that
the said marriage between your Grace and the said Lady
Anne was never good, nor consonant to the laws, but utterly
void and of none effect; by reason whereof your Highness
was, and is lawfully divorced and separated from the bonds
of the same marriage, in the life of the said Anne. And this
notwithstanding most gracious Sovereign Lord, the Lady
Elizabeth, your daughter, being born under the said unlawful marriage, by virtue and authority of the said act of your
succession, above remembered, for lack of heirs males of
your body, should immediately succeed as your lawful heir
in the most royal estate of your Imperial Crown of this realm,
against all honor, equity, reason, and good conscience, if
remedy should not be provided for the same." It then states,

that his Majesty being ignorant of any lawful impediment, entered into the said unlawful marriage with the said Lady Anne, but that she being nevertheless "inflamed with pride and carnal desires, confederated with George Boleyn, late Lord Rochford, her natural brother, Henry Norreys, Esq., Francis Weston, Knight, William Brereton, Gent. and Mark Smeton, and committed most detestable and abominable treasons;" and of which they had been convicted and suffered accordingly: in consequence whereof it is enacted, that the Acts of 25 Hen. VIII. c. 22 and 26 Hen. VIII. c. 2, (the latter of which merely recited part of the former, and ratified the oath to be taken for the due observance of the succession provided by it,) "shall be repeated, annulled, and made frustrate and of none effect." The second clause provides, that such repeal shall not discharge any one from treasons committed against the said Acts; but by the next clause all persons who have spoken or acted against Queen Anne, and her daughter Elizabeth, whereby they may have incurred the peril of Treason under those acts, are declared to be pardoned and released from all penalties of Treason or Misprision. The fourth clause is one of attainder and forfeiture against Queen Anne and her accomplices for Treason. The fifth clause recites, that "for as much as it hath pleased your most royal Majesty, notwithstanding the great and intolerable perils and occasions which your Highness hath suffered and sustained" in former marriages, to enter into marriage again, "and have chosen and taken a right noble, virtuous, and excellent Lady, Queen Jane to your true and lawful wife, and have lawfully celebrated and solemnized marriage with her according to the laws of Holy Church, who for her convenient years, excellent beauty, and pureness of flesh and blood, is apt, (God willing,) to conceive issue by your Highness, which marriage is so pure and sincere, without spot, doubt, or impediment, that the issue procreated under the same, when it shall please God to send it, cannot be lawfully, truly, nor justly interrupted or disturbed of the right in the succession of your Crown." It may therefore, for the prevention of future doubts, &c. please your most gracious Majesty, by consent of the Lords Spiritual and Temporal, and Commons, that it be enacted: "First, that forasmuch as the marriage heretofore solemnized between your Highness and the Lady Katherine, late Princess Dowager, deceased, which afore was lawful wife to your natural brother, Prince Arthur, and by him," &c. (here follow nearly the same words as occur relative to this marriage, in the Act of 25 Hen. VIII. c. 22.) and that the said marriage "shall be by authority of this present Parliament, definitively, clearly, and absolutely declared, deemed, and adjudged to be against the laws of Almighty God, and also accepted, reputed, and taken of no value nor effect, but utterly void and adnichiled," and also, "that the issue born and procreated under the same unlawful marriage made and solemnized between your Highness and the said Lady Katherine, shall be taken, deemed, and accepted, illegitimate, to all intents and purposes, and shall be utterly forclosed, excluded, and barred to claim, challenge, or demand any inheritance as lawful heir to your Highness by lineal descent." It is then by the following clause provided, "that the marriage between your Highness, and the late Queen Anne, shall be taken, reputed, deemed, and adjudged to be of no force, strength, virtue, nor effect,"—"and that all the issues, and children born and procreated under the same marriage, between your Highness and the said late

Queen Anne, shall be taken, reputed, and accepted to be
illegitimate, to all intents and purposes, and utterly forclosed, excluded, and barred to claim, challenge, or demand any inheritance as lawful heir or heirs to your Highness by lineal descent, the said former Act made in the last
Parliament, for the establishment of your succession, or any
thing therein contained, or any other thing or things contrary
thereof, in any wise notwithstanding." The next clause,
like Statute 25 Hen. VIII. cap. 22, relates to the prohibited
degrees of marriage, and it is then enacted: "that all the
issue hereafter to be had and procreate between your Highness and your said most dear and entirely beloved lawful
wife, Queen Jane, shall be your lawful children and heirs,
and be inheritable and inherit according to the course of
inheritance and laws of this realm, the Imperial Crown."
The limitation then follows in nearly the same words as the
Crown was limited to the issue of the King by Queen Anne
Boleyn, namely, to each of his sons by Queen Jane, and their
heirs successively and respectively; in default of which, to
his sons by any other lawful wife, and the heirs of their
bodies; failing which "to the issue female between your Majesty and your said most dear and entirely beloved wife,
Queen Jane begotten, and for lack of such issue, then to
the heirs female of your body lawfully begotten by any
other lawful wife." It is next provided that as it is uncer-
tain whether his Majesty would have issue by his said wife
Queen Jane, and in default of his issue by any other lawful
wife, and no provision being made in his life-time who
should succeed to the Crown, and as it might be dangerous
for him then to name a successor, in default of issue of his
body, lest it might happen that the person so named might,
"take great heart and courage, and by presumption fall to

inobedience and rebellion, by occasion of which premises
great division and dissention, may be and is very likely to
arise and spring in the realm, to the great peril and destruction of us your most humble and obedient subjects, and of
all our posterities, if remedy for the same should not be provided," they putting all their whole trust and confidence in
his Highness, pray that it may be enacted, "That your
Highness shall have full and plenar power and authority to
give, dispose, appoint, assign, declare, and limit by your
letters patent under your great seal, or else by your last will
made in writing, and signed with your most gracious hand,
at your only pleasure, from time to time hereafter, the Imperial Crown of this realm, and all other the premises thereunto belonging, to be, remain, succeed, and come after your
decease, and for lack of lawful heirs of your body to be
procreated and begotten as is afore limited by this act, to
such person or persons, in possession or remainder, as shall
please your Highness, and according to such estate, and
after such manner, form, fashion, order, and condition, as
shall be expressed, declared, named, and limited in your
said letters patent, or by your said last will. And we
your most humble and obedient subjects do faithfully promise to your Majesty by one common assent, that after your
decease, and for lack of heirs of your body lawfully begotten, as is afore rehearsed, we our heirs and successors
shall accept and take, love, dread, serve, and all only obey
such person or persons, males or females, as your Majesty
shall give your said Imperial Crown unto by authority of
this Act, and to none other, and wholly to stick to them, as
true and faithful subjects ought to do, to their regal rulers,
governors, and supreme heads."—"And for sure corrobo-
ration," it was further enacted, that such person or persons

as to whom it shall please your Majesty to dispose, limit,
and assign your said Crown, and other the premises thereto
appertaining by your letters patent, or by your last will as
is aforesaid, shall have and enjoy the same after your decease, and for lack of heirs of your body lawfully begotten,
according to such estate, and after such manner, form,
fashion, order, and condition, as shall be thereof expressed,
mentioned, and contained in your said letters patent, or in
your last will, in as large and ample manner as if such person and persons had been your lawful heirs to the Imperial
Crown of this Realm, and as if the same Crown of this
Realm, had been given and limited to them, plainly and
particularly by special names, and sufficient terms and words,
by the full and immediate authority of this your most high
Court of Parliament." The next clause enacts, that if any
of the King's heirs or children usurp against each other, or
if they, or the persons to whom the Crown may be limited
under the powers of this Act, disturb the descent or limitation under this Act, they shall be deemed guilty of High
Treason, and shall forfeit "as well all such right, title, and
interest, that they may claim or challenge in or to the Crown
of this Realm, as heirs by descent, or by reason of any gift
or Act, that shall be done by your Highness, for his or their
advancement, by authority of this Act or otherwise, by any
manner of means, or pretence whatsoever it be."

The next clause provides, that all persons that shall
do any thing to the peril of the King, his heirs, or successors to the Crown, or by words, writing, deed, or act,
procure or do any thing for the "interruption, repeal, or
annullation of this act," or of the King's dispositions by
force thereof; or to the prejudice of his marriage with
Queen Jane, or of the succession of his issue, or successors

under this act, or of their fame, persons, or title, or shall
judge the King's former marriages with the Lady Katherine, or the Lady Anne, to be valid, or shall impugn the
divorces pronounced against such marriage, or shall call
the children of such marriages legitimate, or under any
pretence shall attempt to deprive the King or his heirs or
successors of title or power, or on being required shall refuse to answer interrogatories on oath, relating to this act,
all such persons shall be adjudged high traitors, and shall
suffer death, and forfeit all their lands and goods.　The remaining clauses provide, that offenders in treason under
this act shall not have privilege of sanctuary; that upon
the King's demise, issue male under eighteen, or issue
female, capable of inheriting the Crown, unmarried under
sixteen years of age, shall be under the guardianship of
their mother and a Council, or a Council only as the
King's will shall direct, and that all persons opposing the
same, shall be deemed guilty of High Treason; that all
subjects shall be sworn to the performance of this act; that
all persons suing livery out of the King's hands, shall take
the said oath, and that those refusing to do so, or protesting
"when they shall be examined upon any interrogatories,
that shall be objected to them, for or concerning this Act,
or any thing therein contained, that they be not bound to
declare their thoughts and conscience, and stifly therein
abide," shall be adjudged guilty of High Treason; that if
the King at any time by his letters patent or will, shall advance any person or persons of his most royal blood, to any
title or dignity, and grant them any estate, such patent or
will shall be as valid as if specified in this act, and as if
granted by authority of Parliament; "And be it finally
enacted by authority aforesaid, that this present Act, and

every clause, article and sentence comprised in the same, shall be taken and accepted according to the plain words and sentences herein contained, and shall not be interpreted nor expounded by colour of any pretence or cause, or by any subtle arguments, inventions, or reasons, to the hindrance, disturbance, or derogation of this act, or any part thereof; any thing or things, act or acts of Parliament, heretofore made, or hereafter to be had, done, or made to contrary thereof notwithstanding; and that every act, statute, law, provision, thing, and things heretofore had or made, or hereafter to be had, done, or made contrary to the effect of this Statute, shall be void, and of no value nor force."

Queen Jane Seymour died 12 October, 1537, and according to the provisions of the stat. 28 Hen. VIII. just recited, her son Prince Edward, was the undoubted heir to the throne; but about May, 1543, immediately after the king's marriage with his sixth and last wife Katherine Parr, another statute, viz. 35 Hen. VIII. cap. 1, was, from the motives assigned in the preamble, passed to regulate the succession, and of which the following is an abstract. The most singular part of it is, that although Mary and Elizabeth were included in the limitation of the crown, they are described only as the king's daughters, without the slightest reference to the proceedings which had annulled the marriages of their respective mothers; and indeed without any allusion to the question of the legitimacy of their births. Hence it would appear that though the crown was on a certain contingency to vest in them and the heirs of their bodies, they were still in fact illegitimate, for it can scarcely be contended that the circumstance of their being described as the king's

daughters would be construed to repeal the solemn act of the
25 and 28 Hen. VIII. by which they had both been expressly
bastardized.

The preamble recites the statute of 28 Hen. VIII. c. 7.
and states that since the making of that act, his Majesty
had only issue of his body lawfully begotten, betwixt his
Highness and his said late wife, Queen Jane, the noble and
excellent Prince Edward, whom Almighty God long preserve; that his Majesty had since the death of Queen Jane
taken to his wife the most virtuous and gracious Lady Katherine, now Queen of England, late wife of John Nevile,
Knt. Lord Latimer, deceased, by whom as yet his Majesty
had no issue, "but may have full well when it shall please
God;" and forasmuch "as our most dread Sovereign Lord
the King, upon good and just ground and causes, intendeth
by God's grace to make a voyage royal, in his royal person
unto the realm of France, against his ancient enemy the
French King, his Majesty most prudently and wisely calling to his remembrance how this realm standeth at this present time, in the case of succession, acknowledging that it
is the only pleasure and will of Almighty God, how long
his Highness or his entirely beloved son Prince Edward
shall live, and whether the said Prince shall have heirs of
his body lawfully begotten or not, or whether his Highness
shall have heirs begotten and procreated between his Majesty
and his said most dear and entirely beloved wife Queen Katherine, that now is, or any lawful heirs and issues of his own
body, begotten by any other his lawful wife, and albeit that
the King's most excellent Majesty, for default of such heirs
as be inheritable by the said act, might by authority of the
said act give and dispose the said Imperial Crown, and other
the premises by his letters patent under his great seal, or

t

by his last will in writing signed with his most gracious
hand, to any person or persons of such estate therein as
should please his Highness to limit and appoint, yet to the
intent that his Majesty's disposition and mind therein should
be openly declared, and manifestly known and ratified, as
well to the Lords Spiritual and Temporal, as to all other
his loving and obedient subjects of this his realm, to the
the intent that their assent and consent might appear to
concur with thus far as followeth of his Majesty's declaration in this behalf: his Majesty therefore thinketh convenient afore his departure beyond the seas, that it be enacted
by his Highness with the assent of the Lords Spiritual and
Temporal, and the Commons in the present Parliament assembled, and by the authority of the same, and therefore be
it enacted by authority aforesaid, that in case it shall
happen the King's Majesty, and the said excellent Prince,
his yet only son, Prince Edward, and heir apparent, to decease without heir of either of their bodies lawfully begotten, (as God defend,) so that there be no such heir, male
or female, of their two bodies to have and inherit the said
Imperial Crown and other his dominions according and in
such manner and form as in the aforesaid act, and now in
this is declared, that then the said Imperial Crown, and
other the premises shall be to the Lady Mary, the King's
Highness daughter, and to the heirs of the body of the same
Lady Mary, lawfully begotten with such conditions as by
his Highness shall be limited by his letters patent, under
his great seal, or by his Majesty's last will in writing,
signed with his gracious hand; and for default of such issue,
the said Imperial Crown, and other the premises, shall be to
the Lady Elizabeth, the King's second daughter, and to the
heirs of the body of the said Lady Elizabeth, lawfully be-

gotten with such conditions as by his Highness shall be
limited by his letters patent under his great seal, or by his
Majesty's last will in writing, signed with his gracious
hand; any thing in the said act, made in the xxviijth year
of our said Sovereign Lord, to the contrary of this act, notwithstanding." The next clauses provide, that on breach
of the conditions which may be imposed by his Majesty, the
crown shall come to the Lady Elizabeth, as though the said
Lady Mary were then dead without heirs of her body, and
that if the said Lady Mary do keep and perform such conditions, and that the said Lady Elizabeth for her part, do
not keep and perform such conditions, the crown shall, for
lack of heirs of the several bodies of the King's Majesty,
the said Lord Prince, and of the said Lady Mary, lawfully
begotten, come to the persons limited by the King's letters
patent, or by his will shall limit and appoint; that on
failure of issue of Lady Elizabeth, and breach of conditions by Lady Mary, the crown shall come to such person as shall be appointed by the King in manner aforesaid; that if no condition be limited by his Majesty, the
estate of the Lady Mary and Lady Elizabeth in the crown,
shall be absolute. By the sixth clause in the act, the King
is empowered to limit the succession of the crown in rever-
sion or remainder by patent or will in case of failure of issue
of the Ladies Mary and Elizabeth, in nearly the same words
as similar power was vested in him by statute 28 Hen. VIII.
c. 7. The seventh, eighth, and ninth clauses, relate to
oaths ordered to be taken by statute 28 Hen. VIII. c. 10,
against the authority of the See of Rome, and provide another oath to be taken instead thereof. The tenth clause
enacts, that persons doing any thing by words, writing,
printing, or by any exterior act or deed tending to procure

the repeal, &c. of this act, or to the interruption, &c. of any limitation of the crown, &c. under this act, shall be declared guilty of High Treason.

The following is a copy of that part of Henry the Eighth's Will, dated 30th December, in the 38th year of his reign, 1546, which related to the succession, and which under the operation of the statutes 28th and 35th, Hen. VIII. on that subject, was of unquestionable authority.

" And as for and concerning the order and disposition of the Imperial Crown of these realms of England, Ireland, with our title of France, and all dignities, honors, &c. for the sure establishment of the succession of the same, and also for a full declaration, limitation, &c. with which conditions our daughters Mary and Elizabeth, shall severally hold, use, and enjoy the said Imperial Crown after our decease, and for default of issue of our son Prince Edward lawfully begotten and his heirs; and also for a full declaration, limitation, &c. to whom, and in which manner, form, and condition, the said Imperial Crown shall remain, and come after our decease; and for default of issue, and heirs of the several bodies of us, our said son Prince Edward, and of our said daughters Mary and Elizabeth, lawfully begotten, we by these presents make and declare our last will and testament concerning the Imperial Crown, in manner and form following: that is to say, immediately after our decease, our said son Prince Edward, shall have, and enjoy, the said Imperial Crown, realm of England, Ireland, our title of France, with all dignities, honors, præeminences, &c. to him and his heirs of his body lawfully begotten; and for default of such issue, we will that the said Imperial Crown, &c. after our two deceases shall wholly remain and come to the heirs of our body lawfully begotten of

the body of our entirely beloved wife, Queen Katherine,[a] that
now is, or of any other our lawful wife, that we shall hereafter
marry for each of such issue and heirs: and for default of issue
of our said son Prince Edward; the said Imperial Crown, &c.
shall wholly remain, and come to our said daughter Mary, and
the heirs of her body lawfully begotten, upon condition that
our said daughter Mary, after our decease shall not marry
without the consent of the Privy Counsellors and others appointed by us to our dearest son Prince Edward aforesaid, to
be of council, or of the most part of them, or of the most part of
them as shall be then alive, thereunto had before the said marriage in writing sealed with their seals; all which conditions
we declare, limit, appoint, and will by these presents, shall be
knit and invested to the said estate of our daughter Mary, in
the said imperial Crown and all other the premises. And if it
fortune our said daughter do die, without lawful issue we will
that the said Imperial Crown, and other the premises shall
wholly remain, and come to our said daughter Elizabeth, and
to the heirs of her body, lawfully begotten, upon condition
that she do not marry, &c." as is just stated, with respect to
her sister Mary. "If it so happen, that our said daughter
Elizabeth do die without lawful issue, and for default of
issue of the bodies of us, of our said son Prince Edward,
and our said daughters, Mary and Elizabeth, the said Imperial
Crown shall wholly remain, and come to the heirs of the
body of the Lady Frances,[b] our niece, eldest daughter to our
late sister the French Queen,[c] lawfully begotten; and for de-

---

[a] Queen Katherine Parr, Henry's sixth and last wife.

[b] Wife of Henry Grey, Duke of Suffolk, and mother of Lady Jane
Grey.

[c] Mary Tudor, Henry's *youngest* sister; she married first Louis
XII. King of France, by whom she had no issue, and secondly,
Charles Brandon, Duke of Suffolk.

fault of such issue of the body of the said Lady Frances, we
will that the said Imperial Crown, and other the premises,
shall wholly remain, and come to the heirs of the body of the
Lady Eleanor our niece, second daughter to our said late sister, the French Queen[a] lawfully begotten; and if it so happen
that the said Lady Eleanor die without issue, then we will
that the said Imperial Crown shall come to our next rightful
heirs. Also we will that if the said Lady Mary marry without
the consent before described, the said Imperial Crown shall
wholly remain to our said daughter Elizabeth, in the same
manner as if the said Lady Mary were then dead without any
lawful issue; and if the said Lady Elizabeth do not marry
according to the said conditions, then that the said Imperial
Crown shall wholly remain to the heirs of the said Lady
Frances, as if the said Lady Elizabeth were then dead without
lawful issue."[b]

No other act of Parliament passed relating to the succession, until the 1st Edward VI. when by statute 1 Edw.
VI. cap. 12, alluded to in page xxxiii. of this volume, for
the repeal of certain statutes concerning Treasons, Felo-
nies, &c. it was by the eighth clause provided, "That if
any of the heirs of the King our said Sovereign Lord that
now is, or any person or persons to whom the crown and
dignity of this realm is limited and appointed by act of
Parliament made in the xxxvth year of the reign of the
said late King Henry the Eighth, or the heirs of any of
them, do at any time hereafter usurp the one of them upon

[a] She married Henry Clifford, Earl of Cumberland, K. G. and left
issue. *Vide the Genealogical Table.*

[b] *Testamenta Vetusta*, Vol. I. pp. 37, 39.

the other in the crown of this realm, or demand, challenge, or claim the same, otherwise, or in any other form or degree of descent or succession, or in any other course, form, degree, or condition, but only in such manner and form as is declared by the said statute, or if any of the said heirs or persons aforesaid do attempt or let the King's Highness that now is peaceably and quietly, to keep, have, and enjoy the said Imperial Crown, that then all and singular, the offenders, their aiders, comforters, abettors, procurers, and counsellors therein, shall be deemed and adjudged High Traitors, and shall suffer and incur the pains of death, losses, and forfeitures, as is aforesaid, in cases of High Treason."

Thus, at the period when Lady Jane Grey usurped the royal dignity, Mary had not only a superior claim under the stat. 35 Hen VII. cap. 7. and under Henry the Eighth's will, but that statute had been solemnly ratified by the act of Parliament 1 Edw. VI. just noticed, and the penalties of High Treason were denounced against all who should attempt to disturb the order of succession provided by it; and it was under this statute, that both Jane and her partizans suffered. The only possible considerations which, therefore, can be urged in favour of her claim was the fact, that at the period when Edward VI. died, both the princesses were by express legislative enactments illegitimate, and that the very statute which settled the crown on them, did not remove the stain of bastardy which had been fixed upon them. Still however, the attempt to place her on the throne was an undoubted act of treason, though attended by more palliating circumstances, than perhaps ever accompanied any previous usurpation. Immediately after Mary's accession, an act passed to repeal the statutes which had legalized her mother's

divorce and her own illegitimacy; the preamble to which,
thus commences, "Forasmuch as truth, being of her own
nature of a most excellent virtue, efficacy, force, and
working, cannot but by process of time break out and shew
herself, howsoever for awhile she may, by the iniquity and
frailty of man, be suppressed and kept close, and being re-
vealed and manifested, ought to be embraced, &c." it is
enacted, that the marriage between the late King Henry shall
be true and valid; the sentence of divorce is declared void;
the statute of 25 Hen. VIII. c. 22, and so much of stat. 28 Hen.
VIII. c. 7, as illegitimates Queen Mary, is declared void and
rendered of no effect, as if it "had never been had, nor
made."

This statute of course confirmed the illegitimacy of the
Princess Elizabeth, for as by it the divorce of Henry from
Katherine of Arragon was annulled, and all proceedings on
the subject absolutely repealed, no marriage between Henry
and any other woman could be considered valid until after
the death of Katherine. That event did not take place until
January 1536, and Queen Elizabeth was born 7 September,
1553, consequently whilst the statute of 1 Mary, cap. 1, remains unrepealed, Elizabeth cannot be deemed to have been
born in lawful wedlock. Though sensible of this circumstance, the act passed on her accession, stat. 1 Eliz. cap. 3.
in no degree bore on the point, further than to acknowledge
that she was "rightly, lineally, and lawfully descended from
the blood royal," and that the crown was undoubtedly vested
in her person; the question of the validity of her mother's
marriage, and the provisions of former statutes on the subject
not being in the slightest degree alluded to. The statute
1st Eliz. cxxiii. which enacted that her majesty should

thenceforth "be enabled in blood, and be inheritable according to the due order and course of the common laws of this your realm to the late Queen Anne your Highness's mother, and to all other your majesty's ancestors and cousins of the part of your said mother; and that as much of every act, record, sentence, judgment, &c. whatsoever, as is, or shall be hereunto contrary or repugnant, shall be from henceforth clearly and utterly void and none effect," proves that the stat. 1 Eliz. c. 3, was not considered to have legalized her birth; nor, it is contended, was that effect produced even by the act in question, which like the preceding, cautiously avoided any allusion to that delicate point.

The preamble to stat. 1 Eliz. c. 3, just alluded to, merely expresses the cause the nation has to rejoice that it has pleased God to preserve her Royal Majesty, their most rightful and lawful sovereign liege Lady and Queen, most happily to reign over them, and states, that it is acknowledged by the Lords Spiritual and Temporal, and the Commons in full Parliament assembled "that your Highness is rightly, lineally, and lawfully descended and come of the blood royal of this realm, in and to whose princely person and the heirs of your body, lawfully to be begotten after you, without all doubt, ambiguity, scruple, or question, the imperial and royal estate, place, crown, and dignity of this realm, with all honors, &c. are and shall be most fully, rightfully, really, and entirely invested and incorporated, united, annexed, &c. to all intents and purposes, as the same were in the said late King Henry the Eighth, or in the late King Edward's the Sixth, your Highnesses brother, or in the late Queen Mary, your Highnosses sister, at any time since the act of Parliament made in the xxxvth year of the reign of your said most noble father King Henry the Eighth, entitled,

u

&c.;" and the limitation of the crown, under stat. 35 Hen.
VIII. c. 1, is declared perpetual, and all sentences, &c. to
the contrary void.

During the long reign of Queen Elizabeth, the only
measure taken on the subject of the succession, was in 1571,
when by statute 13.Eliz. it was declared to be High Treason
to deny the Queen's title, or to call her a heretic; also for
any claimant, during the Queen's life, to pretend to any
right of succession contrary to the Queen's proclamation, or
to deny the power of the common law, or of this or any
other act to limit the descent of the crown; and after the
Queen's decease the same offences were declared to be pu-
nishable with forfeiture of goods; also that persons printing
or publishing during the life of the Queen, that any person,
before the same is by act of Parliament declared, is heir to
the throne, shall for the first offence suffer one year's imprisonment, &c.; and for the second incur the penalties of
the statute of premunire. This act did not, however,
repeal or alter the statute of 35th Hen. VIII. on the subject; hence at her death in 1603, as that statute had been
not only unrepealed, but ratified and confirmed by stat.
1 Eliz. cap. 3, above noticed, the heir to the throne
agreeable to its provisions, was Edward Seymour, com-
monly called Lord Beauchamp, now represented by the present Duchess of Buckingham and Chandos, he being heir
of the body of Frances Brandon, Duchess of Suffolk;* but
James the Sixth of Scotland, being according to the ancient
course of descent of the Crown the undoubted heir to the
Imperial Dignity, his right was at once recognized by the
nation, and confirmed by a statute passed immediately after

* *Vide the Genealogical Table.*

his accession, namely, in the Parliament which met at
Westminster 19th March, 1st Jaq. anno. 1604, entitled "A
most just recognition of the immediate lawful and undoubted
succession, descent, and right of the crown," which alludes
to the union of the houses of York and Lancaster; describes
his majesty's descent from the eldest daughter of King
Henry VII.; recognizes that immediately upon Queen
Elizabeth's death, the crown of England descended to King
James by lawful birth-right and descent; and declares "that
his majesty is of the realms and kingdoms of England,
Scotland, France, and Ireland, the most potent and mighty
king; and by God's goodness more able to protect and
govern us your loving subjects in all peace and plenty, than
any of your noble progenitors."

From the preceding abstracts and observations, the
following curious historical facts may be deduced.

1st. That by two acts of Parliament (25th and 28th
Hen. VIII.) Queen Mary was solemnly bastardized ;

2nd. That the act of 1st Mary which established the
purity of her birth, bastardized her half sister Elizabeth ;
and which had also previously been done by her father by
stat. 28th Hen. VIII.

3rd. That neither the statute 35th Hen. VIII. (nor that
of the 1st Edw. VI. by which its provisions were confirmed)
which included the Princesses Mary and Elizabeth in the
limitation of the crown, rendered either of them *legitimate.*

4th. That Queen Elizabeth was at the time of her decease, in fact, *a bastard.*

5th. And that according to the existing legislative enactments when James the First ascended the throne, and
until the statute was passed which recognized his right to it,
a period of about nine months, i. e. from 24 May, 1603, to

March, 1604, that monarch was a *usurper;* and his partizans which indeed included nearly the whole population of the kingdom, *Traitors!*

ERRATA.

p. lxx, l. 27, for "awere," read "aware."
p. lxxlii, l. 25, for "charge," read change."
p. lxxvi, l. 16, *dele* the word "too."
p. lxxix, l. 2, for "their," read "the."
p. cvi, line last, for "*Britannia,*" read "*Britannica.*"
          Place the Genealogical Table, p. xxx.

THE REMAINS

OF

LADY JANE GREY.

I̅MORTALES tibi ago gratias agamque dum vivam Vir doctissime! nam relaturam me affirmare non possum, tantis enim tuis officiis non videor mihi respondere posse, nisi forte ita censurus es, ut me referre gratiam putes, cum memoria tenebo. Neque i̅merito. Accepi enim a te literas gravissime & disertissime scriptas, quæ quidem mihi gratissimæ erant, tum quod rebus gravioribus omissis ad me, quæ tam eruditi viri literis indigna sum, scribere e tam longinqua regione hac tua ingravescente ætate dignatus es, tum etiam quod ejus generis tua scripta sunt, ut non vulgaria quædam ad delectandum sed pia & divina ad docendum, monendum & consulendum, ea præsertim, quæ & meæ ætati & sexui & familæ nostræ dignitati imprimis conveniunt, continere videantur, in quibus, ut in aliis omnibus, quæ in su̅mam Republicæ Christianæ utilitatem ædidisti, non solum te exquisite doctum & singulari eruditione præditum ostendisti; sed etiam ingeniosum, prudentum & pium consiliarium, qui nihil sapis, nisa bona, nihil sentis, nisi divina, nihil jubes, nisi utilia & nihil paris, nisi honesta, pia & tam observando patre digna. O me felicissimam! cui talis contigit amicus & prudens consiliarus, nam ut Sehlomo habet ברב יעץ ותשועה,[a] quæque jam cum homine tam docto, Theologo tam pio & veræ religionis acerrimo προμαχω necessitudinis & amicitiæ jure conjuncta sum. Multis de nominibus Deo Optimo Maximo me debere puto, & inprimis quod, postquam me pio Bucero viro doctissimo & patre sanctissimo orbasset, qui dies noctesque πυξ και λαξ non destitit mihi, quæ ad vitam instituendam & formandam necessaria essent, suppeditare, quique meum in omni probitate, pietate & literarum scientia cursum & progressus provehebat & suis optimis consiliis adhibitis incitabat: te Vir colendissime! mihi ejus loco concessit, qui ut spero, mihi tardanti, & moram trahenti calcaria, ut cœpisti, addere volueris, nihil enim mihi optatius evenire aut accidere potest, quam ut digna hujus modi clarissimorum virorum, quorum virtutum nullus satis esse possit præco, literis saluberrimisque consiliis ducar, utque idem mihi contingat, quod

---

[a] Prov. xi. 14, Salus in multitudine consilariorum.

vel Blesillæ, Paulæ & Eustachiæ, quas divus ille,
ut fertur, Ieronymus instituit, & suis concionibus
habitis ad divinarum rerum cognitionem perduxit,
vel quod mulieri illi ætate confectæ, cui divus
Joannes epistolium quoddam hortatorium & vere
theologicum conscripsit, vel quod Severi matri,
quæ consilio Originis usa est, ejusque monitis
acquievit, quæ omnes non tantum sibi laudis &
commodi ex corporis forma, generis nobilitate,
& divitiarum copia comparaverunt, quantum
gloriæ & felicitatis ex prudentissimorum virorum
consiliis hauserunt, eo quod non indignabantur
homines illi tam singulari eruditione & admirabili
pietate conspicui eas quasi manu ad optima quæque
ducere & quæ ad salutem æternam & futuræ vitæ
felicitatem maximum haberent momentum sug-
gerere. Quod ut tu mihi facere digneris, cum
neque ingenio nec eruditione, nec pietate infimus
inter eos omnes haberi debeas, iterum atque
iterum a te peto. Audacula tibi videar oportet,
quæ tam audacter hoc efflagito; sed si consilii mei
rationem respicere volueris, nempe quod expie-
tatis tuæ penu ea depromere cupiam, quæ cum
ad mores formandos, tum ad fidem in Christo
Servatore meo confirmandam conducere queant,
hoc quod facio, mihi vitio vertere, nec pro tua
humanitate poteris, nec pro tua prudentia volueris.
Ex libello illo veræ & non fucatæ religionis pleno,

quem nuper ad patrem & me misisti, tanquam ex-
horto amœnissimo flores suavissimos quotidie
colligo, & pater etiam, dum per gravissima negotia
licet, in ejus lectione sedulo versatur, quem
autem inde uteque reportabimus fructum de eo
tibi & Deo propter te immortales gratias agere
debemus : Non enim æquum esse putamus, ut per
te tuique similes, quos non paucos hac in parte
felicissima parit Germania, a Deo Optimo Maximo
tot tantaque vere divina dona ingratis accipiamus
animis. Solemus enim homines hominibus, ut
par est, beneficiis beneficia compensare, & dono-
rum, collatorum memores nos præstare : quanto
magis igitur operam navare debemus divinæ
bonitati, si non ex omni parte respondere, at
saltem lætis animis, quæ confert, amplecti, & ex
animo pro illis gratias agere ?

Nunc ad laudes, quas mihi tribuunt tuæ literæ,
venio, quas ut nec vendicare, ita nullo modo
agnoscere debeo; sed quicquid mihi divina bonitas
largita est, id omne acceptum illi refero, tanquam
mearum rerum omnium, quæ virtutis aliquam
speciem habent, authori summo & soli, quem
meo nomine roges velim ornatissime Vir! assiduis
tuis precibus, ut me in hac parte measque
rationes omnes ita moderetur, ut tanta ejus
benignitate non indigna reperiar. In animum
induxerat illustrissimus pater meus ad tuam

humanitatem scribere pariterque gratias agere
pro tuis præclaræ susceptis laboribus & singulari
illa humanitate, qua inductus es suo nomini,
Quintam Dec. inscribere ejusque auspiciis in
lucem ædere; nisi gravissimis regiæ Majestatis
negotiis in ultimos Britanniæ fines fuissit avoca-
tus, sed ubi per publicas occupationes vacabit,
quam diligentissimé ad te scibere se velle
affirmat. Postremo hebraicari jam incipienti
mihi, si viam & modum aliquem ostenderis, quem
in hoc studiorum cursu tenere maxima cum
utilitate debeam, me longe tibi devinctissimam
reddideris. Vale totius Ecclesiæ Christianæ
summum decus & ornamentum & te diu nobis
suæque Ecclesiæ superstitem servet Deus Optimus
Maximus.

Tuæ pietati deditissima

JωANNA GRAIA.

[TRANSLATION.]

LEARNED Sir, I give you, as I shall continue to
do while I live, unceasing thanks; but cannot
engage ever to requite your kindness, since it
does not appear, that I possess the ability of
making suitable returns for it; unless, indeed,
you should be of opinion, that I return a favour
while I treasure it in memory. These pro-

fessions of gratitude are not made without cause.
I have received from you a profound and eloquent
epistle, which has proved highly grateful to me,
not only in regard to your condescension in
writing from a distant country, and under the
pressure of years, to me who am unworthy of
your notice; but also because your writings are of
no ordinary cast, not calculated merely to amuse,
but abound in pious and divine thoughts, fit for
instruction, admonition and consolation, and
especially suited to my age, sex and rank in life.
In this epistle, as in all those which you have
published to the edification of the Christian community, you have shewn yourself not only a
scholar of singular erudition, but also a skilful,
prudent, and pious counsellor, a man who can
relish nothing which is not excellent; think
nothing which is not divine; enjoin nothing
which is not profitable; and do nothing which is
not virtuous, pious, and worthy of so venerable
a father. O happy me, who am favoured with
such a friend, and so wise a counsellor! for as
Solomon says ותשועה ברב יעץ,ᵃ and who am
connected by the ties of friendship and intimacy,
with so pious a divine, and so intrepid a champion of true religion. On many accounts, I con-

> In the multitude of counsellors there is safety. Prov.
xi. 14.

sider myself indebted to God, the greatest and
best of beings, but especially for having, after I
was bereaved of the pious Bucer, that most
learned man and holy father, who night and day,
and to the utmost of his ability, supplied me with
all necessary instructions and directions, and by
his advice promoted and encouraged my progress
in probity, piety, and learning; for having I say,
granted me in his place, a man so worthy to be
revered as yourself, who, I hope, will continue
as you have begun, to spur me on, when I loiter,
or am inclined to delay. No better fortune can,
indeed, await me, than to be thought worthy of
the wise and salutary admonitions of men so
renowned, whose virtues, who shall sufficiently
eulogize? and to experience the happiness enjoyed
by Blesilla, Paula, and Eustachia, to whom the
divine Jeronymus imparted instruction, and who
were brought by his discourses to a knowledge
of sacred truths—or the happiness of the aged
lady, to whom the divine John addressed an ex-
hortatory and truly evangelical epistle—or lastly,
the happiness of the mother of Severus, who
profited by the lessons of Origen and was obedient to his precepts. These worthies were not
so much honoured and celebrated for beauty of
person, exalted rank, and large possessions, as
their glory and happiness were promoted by the

instructions of wise men, who did not disdain,
though singularly illustrious for erudition and
piety, to conduct them as it were, by the hand,
to every thing excellent, and to suggest to their
minds such thoughts, as might conduce to their
eternal salvation and future felicity. That you,
who are not inferior to these wise counsellors
in understanding, learning and piety, will con-
descend to manifest for me a like kindness is my
unceasing petition. My unreserved requests
may carry with them an appearance of boldness,
but when you consider that they originate in a
desire of extracting from the storehouse of your
piety, instruction for the guidance of my conduct,
and for the confirmation of my faith in Christ my Saviour, your goodness cannot, your wisdom will not,
allow you to censure them. From the little volume
of pure and unsophisticated religion, which you
lately sent my father and me, I cull daily, as out
of a delightful garden, the sweetest flowers. My
father also, as far as the pressure of his occupations
allow, is sedulously engaged in the perusal of it.
Whatever benefit, however, either of us may derive from the perusal, we are bound to render
thanks to you and to God on your account, since
it would not be just to receive with ungrateful
minds, benefits so numerous and truly divine, conferred by the supremely good and great God,

through the instrumentality of you and men such
as you; not a few of whom Germany now sends
forth to this glorious work. If it be customary
with mankind, as indeed it ought to be, to return
favour for favour, and to be mindful of benefits,
surely they are more strongly bound to cherish
and express the most ardent gratitude for divine
favours, though they are unable to make adequate
returns.

I now come to that part of your letter
which contains a panegyric on myself. Your
praises, as I cannot claim, so also, I ought not to
allow. Such of my actions as bear the character-
istics of virtue, I must ascribe solely to that great
Being who is the author of all my natural endowments. To Him, O worthy man! may your prayers
be continually directed on my behalf. May He
so direct my thoughts, that I may be found not
unworthy of his great goodness. My noble
father would have written, both to thank you for
the important services in which you are engaged,
and also for your singular politeness in inscribing
with his name and publishing under his auspices,
your tenth decade, had not weighty business of
his majesty the King called him to the remotest
parts of Britain: but as soon as public affairs
afford him leisure, he is determined on writing
to you.

To conclude, as I am now beginning to study
Hebrew, if you can point out the way in which
I may proceed in this pursuit to the greatest ad-
vantage, you will confer on me a great obligation.

Farewell, bright ornament and grace of the
Christian Church. May the supremely great and
good God, long preserve you for us, and his
people.   Your most devoted,

JANE GRAY.

FACERE non possum, ni nimis ingrata, officii
immemor & beneficiis tuis indigna videri velim,
Vir ornatissime! quin in singulas res meritaque
tua, quæ plurima fuerunt, gratias tibi ingentes
agam. Quanquam me hercule & id cum pudore
facio, neque enim tanta necessitudo, quantam tu
mihi tecum esse voluisti, neque tot beneficia a
te in me his prorsus indignam collata, tantumodo
gratiarum actionem videntur, desiderare, neque
ego lubenter pro maximis tuis beneficiis tam vili
orationis munere defungor. Hoc etiam non nihil
angit animum meum, cum ad literas, quas tanto
viro darem excogitandas, quam parum idonea
sim, jam mecum perpendo. Neque certe meis
næniis puerilibusque nugis tuam gravitatem
perturbare, aut tanta barbarie tuæ eloquentiæ
obstrepere vellem aut auderem, nisi & nullo me

alio modo tibi gratificari posse scirem, & de tua
solita satisque perspecta mihi hæmanitate haud
dubitarem.   De literis autem, quas proxime abs
te accepi, sic habeto.   Posteaquam semel atque
iterum (nam semel non videbatur satis) eas
legissem, tantum fructus reportasse ex tuis præ-
claris & vere theoligicis præceptis visa sum,
quantam ex diuturna optimorum autorum lectione
vix eram assequuta.   Suades ut veram since-
ramque in Christo Servatore meo fidem amplectar.
Tibi hac in parte οσον ο Θεος δωσει, enitar satisfa-
cere, sed donum Dei agnosco eam esse, & proinde
tantum polliceri debeo, quantam Dominus im-
pertierit.   Neque tamen cum Apostolis orare de-
sistam, ut eam mihi sua benignitate indies augere
velit.   Huic etiam eam Deo juvante, ut jubes,
adjungam vitæ puritatem, quam meæ heu nimium
infirmæ vires præstare poterunt.   Tu interea pro
tua pietate in oratione tua mei quotidie facias
mentionem rogo.   Ad Hebraicæ linguæ studium
eam ingrediar viam, quam tu fidelissime monstras.
Vale & Deus te in hac suscepta a te provincia
tueatur & provehat æternum.

Tibi ad omnia pietatis officia
paratissima

1552.   JoANNA GRAIA.

[TRANSLATION.]

ACCOMPLISHED MAN! I cannot do otherwise than thank you for your many acts of kindness to me. Were I to neglect this duty, I should be chargeable with the greatest ingratitude, and might seem forgetful of your goodness and unworthy of your favours. However, I engage in the task with diffidence, for the friendship which you desire to exist between us, and the many favours which you have conferred on me, demand some better return than mere thanks: and I cannot, to the satisfaction of my own mind, discharge by my vain words, the debt of gratitude which I owe you. Moreover, when I direct my thoughts to addressing a letter to a person of your eminence, the consideration of my unfitness for the office not a little disquiets my mind. Nor, indeed, should I wish or presume to trouble your gravity with my trifles and puerilities, or blend my barbarisms with your eloquence, were I not persuaded that I have no other means of gratifying you, and had I not largely experienced your courtesy.

With respect to the letter I have lately received from you—after I had read it once and again (for one perusal seemed insufficient), I appeared to derive such benefit from your excellent and

truly divine precepts, as I have scarcely obtained
from a daily perusal of the best writers. You
exhort me to cherish a genuine and sincere faith
in Christ my Saviour. I shall endeavour to
comply with the exhortation as fully as God
may enable me to do; but as I perceive faith to
be his gift, I cannot promise more than he may
enable me to perform. However, I shall not
cease, with the Apostle, to pray, that God will of
his goodness, increase my faith daily. To faith
I shall, as you recommend, and with the divine
blessing, add holiness of life—that measure of it,
at least, which my too feeble powers may enable
me to produce. Do you, in the mean time, in
the spirit of piety, make daily mention of me in
your prayers. I shall engage in that method of
studying the Hebrew, which you have so clearly
pointed out. Farewell! may God regard you in
the task you have undertaken, and prosper you
eternally.

Your most religiously obedient,

JANE GRAY.

SERA officii recordatio reprehendi non debet,
præsertim si nulla negligentia prætermissa est,
Vir doctissime! Longe enim absum, pauci sunt
tabellarii, audio autem sero; sed jam cum eum

habeam γραμμα7οφορον, cujus opera & meæ Tibi,
& tuæ mihi trada solent litteræ, officio meo deesse
non debui, quin ad te scribendo & verbis optarem
optime & re haberem gratiam, quam diligentissime.
Tanta enim tua apud omnes authoritas, tanta in
prædicando, ut audio, gravitas, tantaque, ut, qui
te norunt, referre solent, vitæ integritas, ut tuis
non solummodo dictis, sed etiam vitæ moribus,
tam peregrinæ & exteræ nationes, quam etiam
ea, quam ipse incolis, patria, magis ad bene
beateque vivendum incitentur. Non enim tan-
tummodo, ut Jacobus habet, Evangelii & sacrorum
Dei mandatorum ebuccinator & prædicator di-
ligens, sed ejus etiam effector & operator verus
es, eaque vita præstas, que verbis imperas,
minime Temetipsum fallens. Nec equidem his
similis es, qui externam suam faciem in speculo
considerant, & quamprimum discesserint, qualis
ejus forma fuerit, oblivioni tradunt; sed & vera
& sincera prædicas, & vivendi ratione aliis, ut
id sequantur, quod & jubes & facis, exemplo &
παραδειμαλι es. Sed quid hæc ad tuam gravitatem scribo, cum tanta mea barbaries sit, ut nec
digne tuam pietatem laudare, nec satis vitæ
integritatem encomiis celebrare, nec prout con-
venit, suspiciendam & admirandam doctrinam
enarrare possit? Opus enim esset, ut, si prout
veritas postulat, Te collaudarem, Demosthenis

vel facundiam, vel Ciceronis eloquentiam haberem,
tanta enim tua sunt merita, ut, cum & tempus
satis longum, tum etiam ingenii acumen & ser-
monis elegantiam plus quam puerilem ad ea
explicanda desiderent. Tantum enim in te sibi,
ut apparet, placuit Deus, ut & te suo regno &
huic mundo adaptaverit, in hoc enim terreno
vitæ ergastulo ætatis cursum transigis, quasi
mortuus esses, cum tamem vivis, idque non solum,
primum Christo, sine quo nulla vita esse potest &
deinde tibi, sed etiam infinitis aliis, quos ut ad
eam immortalitatem, quam ipse assecuturus es,
posteaquam ex hac vita migraveris, diis volentibus
perducas, strenue laboras & assidue conaris,
utque id tua pietas effectum reddat, quod cupit,
Deum παντοκρατορα omnium rerum bonarum
largitorem precari non cessabo, ejusque divinas
aures, ut diu in hac vita superstes sis, pulsare
non desinam. Hæc ad te audacius, quam pru-
dentius scripsi, sed tua in me beneficia tanta
extiterunt, qui ad me tibi incognitam scribere &
quæ ad animum ornandum & mentem expoliendam
necessaria essent, suppeditare dignatus es, merito
negligentiæ incusari & officii oblita videri pos-
sem, si omnimodo me tui tuorumque meritorum
memorem haud præberem. Magnaque præterea
mihi spes est, te huic mea plusquam muliebri
audaciæ, quæ virgo ad virum, & indocta ad eru-

ditionis patrem scribere audeam, ignoscere, &
meæ barbariei, quæ te gravioribus rebus occupa-
tùm meis tricis, næniis, & puerilibus literis perturbare non dubitem, veniam dare velle; quodsi
a te impetravero, me multis nominibus tuæ
pietati debere plurimum existimabo. Si quid
enim hac in parte peccatum fuerit, mei erga te
tuasque virtutes amoris abundantiæ potius tri-
buendum est, quam vel audaciæ, quæ in nostram
sexum nullo modo cadere debet, vel temeritati,
quæ *ἰη ἰης πρισεως δυναμει* valde adversari solet,
splendor siquidem tuarum dotum ita mentis meæ
aciem, vel cum tua lego, vel cum de te cogito,
perstringit, ut non, quid meæ conveniat condi-
tioni, sed quid tuæ debeatur dignitati, in mentis
meæ cognitionem veniat. Cæterum hic fluctuare
animus solet, atque in diversas distrahi partes,
dum quid mea ætas, sexus & in literis mediocri-
tas, imo infantia potius postulat, mecum consi-
dero, quæ cum singula, tum universa multo magis
a scribendi officio deterrent. Contra autem,
cum tuarum virtutum præstantiam, famæ tuæ
celebritatem & meritorum tuorum erga me mag-
nitudinem intueor, superior inferiori cogitatio
cedit, *ἰο πρεπον με* dignitati tuæ: & plus apud me,
quod tua postulant merita, quam quod alia suadent
omnia, valere solet. Reliquum autem est, Vir
clarissime! ut vehementer a te petam, meo

nomine viro illi inclito & eruditione, pietate
gravitateque antesignano nomine Bibliandro,
mihi tamen incognito, salutem ex animo dicere.
Tantam enim ejus in nostra patria eruditionis
famam audio, tamque illustre ejus nomen apud
omnes, ob singulares animi dotes a Deo illi con-
cessas esse accipio, ut nolens volens hujusmodi
viri cælitus, nisi fallor, nobis emissi, pietatem
sinceritatemque amplecti quæ paululum cogni-
tionis ipsa consequuta sum, cogar & ut diu hujusmodi Ecclesiæ columnæ, qualis vos estis, pros-
pera sint valetudine Deum precor. Tuæ autem
gravitati bene optare, ob humanitatem mihi osten-
sam gratias agere & multem valere jubere,
quamdiu spirare licuerit, non desinam. Vale vir
doctissime

Tuæ pietati deditissima

1553.   JoANNA GRAIA.

[TRANSLATION.]

THE late observance of a duty ought not, Learned
Sir, to be censured, when not omitted through
neglect. The truth is, I· am far removed from
you, the letter carriers are few, and news reaches
me slowly. As I can now, however, avail myself of the messenger, by whom my letters to you,

D

and yours to me, have been hitherto conveyed, I
must not neglect writing to you, but must, both in
word and deed, discharge an obligation as speedily
as possible.

So great, indeed, is your authority with all
men, such, as I hear, the solidity of your preach-
ing, and such the integrity of your life, according
to the report of those who are acquainted with
you, that foreign and remote people, as well as
your own countrymen, are by your actions, not
less than by your words, incited to follow a good
and happy life. For you are not only, as James
says, a diligent preacher and herald of the gospel
and of the sacred laws of God, but also a genuine
observer and doer of them; and you exhibit, in
your own life that practice which your precepts
enjoin, not deceiving yourself. Nor, indeed, do
you resemble the persons who behold their face
in a glass, and as soon as they have departed,
forget the form of it, but you preach truth and
sincerity, and afford an example of that course,
which you enjoin others to follow. But why do
I thus accost your gravity, when such is my want
of refinement, that I cannot adequately celebrate
your piety and integrity, or in a becoming manner,
display your admirable doctrine. Were I, indeed,
to praise you as truth requires, I should need the
eloquence of Demosthenes and Cicero. Such are

your merits, that to declare them, length of time, acuteness of understanding, and elegance of language beyond that which so young a person can display, are necessary. God appears to have so fitted you, both for his kingdom, and this world, that in this earthly prison you pass your days, as dead to the world; nevertheless you live, not only to Christ, without whom there can be no life, and to yourself, but also to many others, whom you strenuously labour and assiduously endeavour with the divine will, to bring to that immortality which yourself will obtain, when you quit this life. That your piety may render your wishes effectual, is my unceasing prayer to God, the supreme ruler of the universe, and the giver of all good things; whose ears I constantly importune for your long continuance in this life.

In accosting you in this way, I may display more boldness than prudence; but so great has been your condescension in writing to me, a stranger, and in supplying me with instruction for the culture and adorning of my mind, that I should deservedly appear chargeable with neglect and forgetfulness of duty, did I not, to the utmost of my endeavours, treasure up the remembrance of your benefits. Besides, I cherish the hope that you will pardon the more than feminine

boldness of an untaught virgin, who presumes to
write to a man, and one too who is a father in
learning; and that you will overlook that rudeness
which has not hesitated to interrupt your graver
pursuits with nonsensical trifles and puerilities.
Let me but obtain your pardon, and I shall consider myself much indebted to your goodness on
many accounts. If I have, indeed, offended by
this measure, ascribe rather to my exceeding love
of you and of your virtues, than to boldness, which
ought never to exist in our sex, or to rashness,
which obtrudes itself with a saw like power.
The splendour of your endowments so dazzles my
mental perception, whether I read your writings
or contemplate your character, that my thoughts
are occupied in considering, not the behaviour
becoming my condition, but the tribute due to
your excellence. My mind, indeed, fluctuates
and forms different determinations. When I
consider my age, sex, moderate attainments in
literature, and I may add, my infancy, I am
deterred from writing; but when I consider the
eminence of your virtues, the celebrity of your
character, and the magnitude of your favours
towards me, the first consideration yields to the
last—the behaviour becoming me, to the tribute
due to you; the respect which your merits
demand, prevails over all other considerations.

It only remains for me earnestly to beseech you, illustrious Sir, cordially to salute in my name, the excellent Bibliander, that pattern of learning, piety, and seriousness, though he is personally unknown to me. So excellent is the character which he bears in my own country, and so celebrated his name with all people, that I am irresistibly led to seek an acquaintance with a man of such piety and integrity, a man sent us, if I am not deceived, from heaven. I am also urged to pray, that as pillars of the Church you may enjoy good health. As long as I shall be permitted to live, I shall not cease to be your well-wisher, to thank you for your favours, and to pray for your welfare.

Farewell, Learned Sir,

Your most religiously obedient,

1553. JANE GREY.

AN EPISTLE FROM THE LADY JANE GREY TO A NOBLE
FRIEND OF HER'S NEWLY FALLEN FROM THE TRUTH.

So oft as I call to mind (dear friend and
chosen Brother) the dreadful and fearful sayings
of God, that he which layeth hold upon the plough
and looketh back again, is not meet for the kingdom of heaven; and on the other side to remember the comfortable words of our Saviour
Christ, to all those that forsaking themselves do
follow him, I cannot but marvel at thee and lament thy case; that thou, which sometimes wert
the lively member of Christ, but now the deformed
imp of the devil; sometimes the beautiful temple
of God, but now the stinking and filthy kennel of
Satan; sometimes the unspotted spouse of thy
Saviour, but now the unshamefast paramour of
Antichrist; sometimes my faithful brother, but
now a stranger and apostate; yea sometimes my
stout christian soldier, but now a cowardly runa-
way. So oft as I consider the threatenings and
promises of the Divine Justice to all those which
faithfully love him, I cannot but speak to thee,
yea, rather cry out and exclaim against thee,
thou seed of Satan, and not of Juda, whom the
devil hath deceived, the world hath beguiled, and
desire of life hath subverted, and made of a
christian an infidel.

Wherefore hast thou taken upon thee the Testament of the Lord in thy mouth? wherefore hast thou hitherto yielded thy body to the fire, and to the bloody hands of cruel tyrants? wherefore hast thou instructed others to be strong in Christ, when thou thyself dost now so horribly abuse the testament and law of the Lord; when thou thyself, preachest (as it were not to steal) yet most abominably stealest, not from men but from God, and as a most heinous sacrilegious robber, robbest Christ thy redeemer of his right in his members, thy body and thy soul; when thou thyself dost rather choose to live miserably (with shame) in this world, than to die gloriously and reign in honour with Christ, to the end of all eternity, in whom even in death there is life beyond wish, beyond all expression; and when, I say, thou thyself art most weak, thou oughtest to show thyself most strong, for the strength of a fort is known before the assault, but thou yieldest (like a faint captain) thy hold before any battery be brought against thee.

Oh wretched and unhappy man what art thou but dust and ashes, and wilt thou resist thy maker, that formed and fashioned thee: wilt thou now forsake him that called thee from custom-gathering among the Romish Antichristians, to be an ambassador and messenger of his eternal

word; he that first framed thee, and since thy
creation and birth preserved thee, nourished thee,
and kept thee, yea, and inspired thee with the
spirit of knowledge (I cannot, I would I could
say of grace) shall he not possess thee, darest
thou deliver up thy self to another, being not
thine own, but his? How canst thou, having
knowledge; or how darest thou neglect the law of
the Lord, and follow the vain traditions of men?
and whereas thou hast been a public professor
of his name, become now a defacer of his glory.
I will not refuse the true God, and worship the
invention of man, the golden calf, the whore of
Babylon, the Romish religion, the abominable
idol, the most wicked mass: wilt thou torment
again, rent and tear the most precious body of our
Saviour Christ with thy bodily and fleshly teeth
without the breaking whereof upon the cross, our
sins and transgressions, could else no way be re-
deemed? wilt thou take upon thee to offer up any
sacrifice unto God for our sins, considering that
Christ offered up himself (as St. Paul saith) upon
the Cross, a lively sacrifice once for all.

Can neither the punishment of the Israelites
(which for their idolatry so oft they received)
move thee; neither the terrible threatenings of the
ancient prophets stir thee, nor the crosses of
God's own mouth fear thee to honour any other

God than him? wilt thou so regard him that
spared not his dear and only son for thee, so
diminishing, yea, utterly extinguishing his glory,
that thou wilt attribute the praise and honour to
idols, which have mouths and speak not, eyes and
see not, ears and yet hear not, which shall perish
with them that made them: what saith the pro-
phet Baruck, where he reciteth the epistle of
Jeremy, written to the captive Jews? did he not
forewarn them that in Babylon they should see
gods of gold, silver, wood, and stone, borne upon
men's shoulders to cause a fear upon the heathen?
but be not you afraid of them (saith Jeremy) nor
do as others do: but when you see others worship
them, say you in your hearts, it is thou (O Lord)
that oughtest only to be worshipped: for as touching the timber of those gods the carpenter framed
them and polished them, yea guilded they be and
laid over with silver and vain things and cannot
speak: he sheweth moreover, the abuse of their
deckings how the priests took off their ornaments,
and apparelled there women therewithal: how one
holdeth a sceptre, another a sword in his hand,
and yet can they judge in no matter, nor defend
themselves, much less any other, from either
hatred or murder, nor yet from knawing worms,
dust, filth, or any other evil thing; these and such
like words speaketh Jeremy unto them, whereby

E

he proveth them but vain things, and no gods,
and at last he concludeth thus ; confounded be
those that worship them.

They were warned by Jeremy, and thou as
Jeremy hast warned others, and art warned thyself
by many Scriptures in many places.

God, saith he, is a jealous God, which will have
all honour, glory, and worship given to him only.
And Christ saith in the fourth of Luke, to satan
which tempted him, even to the same satan, the
same Belzebub, the same devil which hath prevailed against thee : it is written (saith he) thou
shalt honour the Lord thy God, and him only
shalt thou serve.

These and such like do prohibit thee, and all
Christians to worship any other God than he which
was before all worlds, and laid the foundations both
of heaven and earth, and wilt thou honour a detestable idol invented by the Popes of Rome, and the
uncharitable college of politic Cardinals?

Christ offered up himself once for all, and
wilt thou offer him up again daily at thy pleasure ?
but thou wilt say thou doest it for a good intent:
Oh sink of sin ! Oh child of perdition ! canst thou
dream of any good intent therein, when thy conscience beareth thee witness of the wrath of God
promised against thee?

How did Saul, who for that he disobeyed the

word of God for a good intent, was thrown from
his wordly and temporal kingdom: shalt thou then
which dost so deface God's honour and rob him
of his right, inherit the eternal heavenly kingdom?
wilt thou for a good intent pluck Christ out of
heaven, and make his death void, and deface the
triumph of his cross, offering him up daily? wilt
thou either for fear of death, or hope of life, deny
and refuse thy God, who enriched thy poverty?
healed thy infirmity, and yielded to this victory if
thou wouldst have kept it? dost thou not consider
that the thread of life hangeth upon him that made
thee, who can (as his will is) either twine it hard
to last the longer, or untwine it again to break the
sooner? Dost thou not remember the saying of
David, a notable king, which teacheth thee, a
miserable wretch, in his civ Psalm, where he saith,
When thou takest away thy spirit, O Lord, from
men, they die, and are turned again to their dust,
but when thou lettest thy breath go forth, they
shall be made, and thou shalt renew the face of
the earth.

Remember the saying of Christ in his Gospel,
whosoever seeketh to save his life shall lose it, but
whosoever will lose it for my sake shall find it;
and in another place, whosoever loveth father or
mother above me, is not meet for me, for he that
will be my disciple, must forsake father and

mother, and himself, and take up his cross. and
follow me : what cross? the cross of infamy and
shame, of misery and poverty, of affliction and
persecution, for his name sake.

Let the oft falling of those heavenly showers
pierce thy stony heart; let the two-edged sword
of God's holy word hew asunder the knit-together
sinews of worldly respects, even to the very mar-
row and life blood of thy carnal heart, that thou
mayst once again forsake thyself to embrace
Christ, and like as good subjects will not refuse to
hazard all in the defence of their earthly and temporal governors, so fly not like a white livered
milk-sop from the standard, whereby thy chief
Captain, Christ, hath placed thee in a noble array
of this life; viriliter ago confortetur cor tuum et
sustine dominum, fight manfully, come life, come
death, the quarrel is God's, and undoubtedly the
victory is ours.

But thou wilt say, I will not break unity;
what? not the unity of satan and his members,
not the unity of darkness, the agreement of antichrist and his adherents ? nay, then thou deceives
thyself with fond imaginations of such an unity
as is amongst the enemies of Christ : were not the
false prophets in an unity? were not Joseph's brethren, Jacob's sons, in an unity? were not the
heathen as the Amelechites, the Peresites and

Jebusites in an unity? I keep no order but look rather to my matter: were not the Scribes and Pharisees in an unity? doth not King David testify, conveniunt in unum adversus Dominum, yea, thieves and murderers, conspirators and traitors have their unity.

.Mark my dear friend (yea friend if thou beest not God's enemy,) there is no unity but when Christ knitteth the knot amongst such as be his, yea, be you well assured that where his truth is resident, there it is verified, that he saith, Non veni mittere pacem in terram sed gladium, that is, Christ came to set one against another; the son against the father, the daughter against the mother: deceive not thyself therefore with the glistering and glorious name of unity, for antichrist hath his unity, yet not in deed, but in name, for the agreement of evil men is not an unity, but a conspiracy.

Thou hast heard some threatenings, some curses, and some admonishments of the Scriptures, to those who love themselves above Christ.

Thou hast heard also the sharp and biting words to those which deny him for love of life, saith he not, that he which denieth me before men, I will deny him before my father which is in heaven: and to the same effect writeth St. Paul in the vi. to the Hebrews, saying, it is impossible that

they which have been once lightened, and have
tasted of the heavenly gift of grace, and been made
partakers of the Holy Ghost, and have relished of
the pure word of God, if they fall and slide away,
it is impossible that they should be renewed again
by repentance, crucifying again to themselves the
Son of God, and making him as it were a mocking-
stock, or gaude of their fancies. And again, (saith
he) if we shall willingly sin after we have received
the knowledge of the truth, there is no oblation
left for sin, but the terrible expectation of judgment and fire which shall devour the adversaries.
Thus St. Paul writeth, and thus thou readest, and
dost thou not quake and tremble? well, if these
terrible and thundering alarums cannot stir thee to
arise and cleave unto Christ, and forsake the world,
yet let the sweet consolations and promises of the
Scriptures: let the examples of Christ and his
Apostles, both Martyrs and Confessors, encourage
thee to take faster hold by Christ. Hearken what
he saith again in his holy Gospel; blessed are you
when men revile you, and persecute you for my
sake, rejoice and be glad, for great is your reward
in heaven, for so persecuted they the Prophets
before you.

Hear what Esau saith: fear not the curse of
men, be not afraid of their blasphemies and rail-
ings, for worms and moths shall eat them up like

cloth and wool, but my righteousness shall endure
for ever, and my saving health from generation to
generation: what art thou then (saith he) that
fearest a mortal man, the child of a man, which
fadeth away as doth the flower, and forgettest the
Lord that made thee, that spread out the heavens
like a curtain, and laid the foundations of the
earth so sure, that they cannot be removed: I am
the Lord thy God, which maketh the sea to rage,
and to be still, who is the Lord of hosts; I shall
put my word in thy mouth, and defend thee with
the turning of a hand. And our Saviour Christ
saith to his disciples, they shall accuse you, and
bring you before the princes and rulers for my
name sake, and some of you they shall persecute
and kill: but fear you not (saith he) neither care
you not what you shall say, for it is my spirit that
speaketh in you, the hand of the highest shall
defend you, for the hairs of your heads are num-
bered, and none of them shall perish. I have laid
up treasure for you (saith he) where no thief can
steal, nor moth corrupt, and happy are you if you
endure to the end. Fear not them (saith Christ)
which have power over the body only, but fear
him that hath power both over the body and the
soul; the world loveth her own, and if you were of
the world the world would love you, but you are
mine, and therefore the world doth hate you.

Let these, and such like consolations out of the Scriptures strengthen you to God-ward; let not the examples of holy men and women go out of your mind, as that of Daniel, and the rest of the prophets; of the three children of Eleazarus, that constant father; the Machabees' children, that of Peter, Paul, Stephen, and other Apostles and holy Martyrs, in the beginning and infancy of the Church; as of good Simeon, Archbishop of Seloma, and Zetrophone, with infinite others, under Sapores the king of the Persians and Indians, who condemned all torments devised by the tyrants for their Saviour's sake.

Return, return again for honour and mercy's sake into the way of Christ Jesus, and as becometh a faithful soldier, put on that armour which St. Paul teacheth to be most necessary for a Christian man, and above all things take to you the shield of faith.

And be you most devoutly provoked by Christ's own example, to withstand the devil, to forsake the world, and to become a true and faithful member of his mystical body, who spared not his own flesh for our sins. Throw down thyself with the fear of his threatened vengeance for this so great and heinous offence of apostacy, and comfort yourself on the other part with the mercy, blood, and promises of him that is ready to turn to you when-

soever you turn to him : disdain not to come again
with the lost son, seeing you have so wandered with
him : be not ashamed to turn again with him from
the swill of strangers, to the delicates of the most
benign and loving father, acknowledging that you
have sinned against heaven and earth; against
heaven by staining his glorious name, and causing
his most sincere and pure word to be evil spoken
of through you; against earth by offending your so
many weak brethren to whom you have been a
stumbling block through your sudden sliding.

Be not ashamed to come again with Mary, and
to weep bitterly with Peter, not only with shedding
of tears out of your bodily eyes, but also pouring
out the streams of your heart, to wash away, out
of the sight of God, the filth and mire of your of-
fensive fall; be not ashamed to say with the pub-
lican, Lord be merciful unto me a sinner: remember
the horrible history of Julian of old, and the
lamentable case of Francis Spira of late, whose
remembrance me thinketh should be yet so green
to your memory, that being a thing of our time,
you should fear the like inconvenience, seeing that
you are fallen into the like offence. Last of all,
let the lively remembrance of the last day be
always before your eyes, remembering the terror
that such shall be in at that time, with the runa-
gates and fugitives from Christ, which setting more

F

by the world than by heaven, more by their life,
than by him that gave them their life, more by the
vanity of a painful breath, than the perfect assu-
rance of eternal salvation, did shrink; yea, did
clean fall away from him that never forsook them.
And contrariwise, the inestimable joys prepared for
them which feared no peril, nor dreading death,
have manfully fought, and victoriously triumphed
over all power of darkness; over hell, death, and
damnation, through their most redoubted captain
JESUS CHRIST our Saviour, who even now
stretcheth out his arms to receive you, ready to-
fall upon your neck, and kiss you: and last of all,
to feast you with the dainties and delicates of his
own most precious blood, which undoubtedly, if it
might stand with his determinate purpose, he would
not let to shed again, rather than you should be
lost; to whom with the Father and the Holy
Ghost, be all honour, praise, and glory everlast-
ingly. Amen.

Your's, if you be Christ's,

JANE GREY.

Postscript.

Be constant, be constant, fear not for pain,
Christ hath deliver'd thee, and heav'n is thy gain.

J. G.

A CONFERENCE, DIALOGUE-WISE, HELD BETWEEN THE LADY
JANE DUDLEY AND M. FECKENHAM, FOUR DAYS BEFORE
HER DEATH, TOUCHING HER FAITH AND RELIGION.

FECKENHAM. What thing is required in a
Christian?

JANE. To believe in God the Father, in God
the Son, in God the Holy Ghost, three persons and
one God.

FECKENHAM. Is there nothing else required
in a Christian, but to believe in God?

JANE. Yes: We must believe in him, we must
love him, with all our heart, with all our soul, and
all our mind, and our neighbour as ourself.

FECKENHAM. Why then faith justifieth not,
nor saveth not?

JANE. Yes, verily, faith (as St. Paul saith)
only justifieth.

FECKENHAM. Why St. Paul saith, if I have all
the faith of the world, without love, it is nothing.

JANE. True it is, for how can I love him I
trust not, or how can I trust in him whom I love
not; faith and love ever agree together, and yet
love is comprehended in faith.

FECKENHAM. How shall we love our neighbour?

JANE. To love our neighbour, is to feed the

hungry, clothe the naked, and to give drink to the thirsty, and to do to him as we would do to ourselves.

FECKENHAM. Why, then it is necessary to salvation to do good works, and it is not sufficient to believe?

JANE. I deny that, I affirm that faith only saveth; for it is meet for all Christians, in token that they follow their master Christ, to do good works; yet may we not say, nor in any wise believe, that they profit to salvation: for although we have done all that we can, yet we are unprofitable servants, and the faith we have only in Christ's blood and his merits, saveth.

FECKENHAM. How many Sacraments are there?

JANE. Two: the one the Sacrament of Baptism, and the other the Sacrament of the Lord's Supper.

FECKENHAM. No, there be seven Sacraments.

JANE. By what Scripture find you that?

FECKENHAM. Well, we will talk of that hereafter: but what is signified by your two sacraments?

JANE. By the Sacrament of Baptism I am washed with water, and regenerated in the spirit, and that washing is a token to me that I am the child of God: the Sacrament of the Lord's Supper is offered unto me as a sure seal and testimony, that I am, by the blood of Christ which he shed

for me on the cross, made partaker of the everlasting kingdom.

FECKENHAM. Why, what do you receive in
that bread: do you not receive the very body and
blood of Christ?

JANE. No, surely, I do not believe so: I
think at that supper I receive neither flesh nor
blood, but only bread and wine; the which bread
when it is broken, and the wine when it is drunk,
putteth me in mind how that for my sins the body
of Christ was broken, and his blood shed on the
cross, and with that bread and wine I receive the
benefits which came by breaking of his body, and
by the shedding of his blood on the cross for my
sins.

FECKENHAM. Why but, madam, doth not
Christ speak these words: take eat, this is my
body: can you require any plainer words: doth
he not say, that it is his body?

JANE. I grant he saith so; and so he saith
likewise in other places, I am the vine, I am the
door, it being only but a figurative speech: doth
not St. Paul say that he calleth those things which
are not as though they were? God forbid, that I
should say that I eat the very natural body and
blood of Christ: for then either I should pluck
away my redemption, or confess there were two
bodies, or two Christ's: two bodies, the one body

was tormented on the cross, and then if they did
eat another body, how absurd: again, if his body
was eaten really, then it was not broken upon
the cross, or if it were broken upon the cross (as
it is doubtless) then it was not eaten of his disciples.

FECKENHAM. Why, is it not as possible that
Christ by his power could make his body both to
be eaten and broken, as to be born of a woman
without the seed of man, and as to walk on the
sea having a body, and other such like miracles,
which he wrought by his power only?

JANE. Yes, verily, if God would have done
at his last supper a miracle, he might have done
so: but I say he minded nor intended no work or
miracle, but only to break his body, and shed his
blood on the cross for our sins: but I beseech
you answer me to this one question; where was
Christ when he said, take, eat, this is my body:
was not he at the table? when he said so he was
at that time alive, and suffered not till the next
day; well, what took he but bread? and what
broke he but bread? and what gave he but bread?
look what he took he brake, and look what he
brake he gave, and look what he gave that did
they eat, and yet all this while he himself was at
supper before his disciples, or else they were deceived.

FECKENHAM. You ground your faith upon such authors as say and unsay, both with a breath, and not upon the church, to whom you ought to give credit.

JANE. No, I ground my faith upon God's word, and not upon the church: for if the church be a good church, the faith of the church must be tried by God's word, and not God's word by the church: neither yet my faith: shall I believe the church because of antiquity? or shall I give credit to that church which taketh away from me a full half part of the Lord's Supper, and will not layman receive it in both kinds, but the priests only themselves, which thing if they deny to us part, they deny us part of our salvation? and I say, that it is an evil and no good church, and not the spouse of Christ, but the spouse of the devil, which altereth the Lord's Supper, and both taketh from it, and addeth to it: to that church I say God will add plagues, and from that church will he take their part out of the Book of Life: you may learn of St. Paul, how he did administer it to the Corinthians in both kinds, which since your church refuseth, shall I believe it? God forbid!

FECKENHAM. That this was done by the wisdom of the church, and to a most good intent to avoid an heresy, which then sprung in it.

JANE. O, but the church must not alter God's will and ordinances, for the colour or gloss of a good intent: it was the error of King Saul, and he not only reaped a curse, but perished thereby, as it is evident in the Holy Scriptures.

To this M. Feckenham gave me a long, tedious, yet eloquent reply; using many strong and logical persuasions, to compel me to have leaned to their church: but my faith had armed my resolution to withstand any assault that words could then use against me. Of many other articles of religion we reasoned, but these formerly rehearsed were the chiefest and most effectual.

JANE DUDLEY.

AN EXHORTATION WRITTEN BY LADY JANE DUDLEY, THE
NIGHT BEFORE HER EXECUTION, IN THE END OF THE
NEW TESTAMENT, IN GREEK, WHICH SHE SENT TO
HER SISTER, THE LADY KATHERINE GREY.

I HAVE here sent you, my dear sister Katherine,
a book, which although it be not outwardly trim-
med with gold, or the curious embroidery of the
artfulest needles, yet inwardly it is more worth
than all the precious mines which the vast world
can boast of: it is the book, my only best, and
best loved sister, of the law of the Lord: it is
the Testament and last will, which he bequeathed
unto us wretches and wretched sinners, which
shall lead you to the path of eternal joy: and if
you with a good mind read it, and with an earnest
desire follow it, no doubt it shall bring you to an
immortal and everlasting life: it will teach you to
live, and learn you to die: it shall win you more,
and endow you with greater felicity, than you
should have gained possession of our woeful father's
lands: for as if God had prospered him, you should
have inherited his honours and manors, so if you
apply diligently this book, seeking to direct your
life according to the rule of the same, you shall be
an inheritor of such riches, as neither the covetous
shall withdraw from you, neither the thief shall
steal, neither yet the moths corrupt: desire with

G

David, my best sister, to understand the law of
the Lord your God, live still to die, that you by
death may purchase eternal life, and trust not that
the tenderness of your age shall lengthen your
life : for unto God, when he calleth, all hours,
times and seasons are alike, and blessed are they
whose lamps are furnished when he cometh, for
as soon will the Lord be glorified in the young as
in the old.

My good sister, once more again let me entreat
thee to learn to die; deny the world, defy the
devil, and despise the flesh, and delight yourself
only in the Lord : be penitent for your sins, and
yet despair not; be strong in faith, yet presume
not; and desire with St. Paul to be dissolved and
to be with Christ, with whom, even in death there
is life.

Be like the good servant, and even at midnight be waking, lest when death cometh and
stealeth upon you, like a thief in the night, you
be with the servants of darkness found sleeping;
and lest for lack of oil you be found like the
five foolish virgins, or like him that had not on
the wedding garment, and then you be cast into
darkness, or banished from the marriage : rejoice
in Christ, as I trust you do, and seeing you have
the name of a christian, as near as you can follow
the steps, and be a true imitator of your master

Christ Jesus, and take up your cross, lay your sins on his back, and always embrace him.

Now as touching my death, rejoice as I do, my dearest sister, that I shall be delivered of this corruption, and put on incorruption: for I am assured that I shall, for losing of a mortal life, win one that is immortal, joyful, and everlasting: the which I pray God grant you in his most blessed hour, and send you his all-saving grace to live in his fear, and to die in the true christian faith: from which in God's name I exhort you that you never swerve, neither through hope of life, nor fear of death: for if you will deny his truth, to give length to a weary and corrupt breath, God himself will deny you, and by vengeance make short what you by your soul's loss would prolong: but if you will cleave to him, he will stretch forth your days to an uncircumscribed comfort, and to his own glory: to the which glory, God bring me now, and you hereafter, when it shall please him to call you. Farewell once again, my beloved sister, and put your only trust in God, who only must help you. Amen.

Your loving Sister.

JANE DUDLEY.

ANOTHER COPY OF THIS LETTER HAS LATELY BEEN PRINTED,[a] TAKEN FROM THE BLANK PAGES OF A MANUSCRIPT ON VELLUM, PRESERVED IN THE BRITISH MUSEUM,[b] CONTAINING AN ESSAY BY ALBERTUS CASTELLANUS, "DE ARTE MORIENDI;" AND AS THAT TRANSCRIPT DIFFERS IN A SLIGHT DEGREE FROM THE PRECEDING, ITS INSERTION APPEARS DESIRABLE.

"This exhórtacyon was writen by Lady Jane Dudley to her sister Katherine yᵉ night bifo she suffred:

" I haue sent yō good sustʳ K. a boke wh although it be not outwardly rimid with gold, yet inwardly it is most worth then p̃cyous stones. It is the boke, dere sistʳ, of the laws of the Lord; it is his testament and last will, wch he bequeathed unto us wretches, wch shall lead yō to the path of eternall joye, and yf yō wth a good mĩde reade it, and with an earnest dissyre folow it, shall bring you to an imortale and everlasting lyfe. It wyll teach yō to lyve, and learne yō to dey: it shall wyne yō more then yō sholde haue gayned by the possessyon of yoʳ wofull fathres lands, for as

[a] *Lady Jane Grey and her Times*, p. 372.
[b] Harl. MSS. 2370.

if god had p̃spered him, yō shold haue inherited
his lands, so if yō aply diligẽtly yoʳ boke, trying to directe yoʳ lyfe aftʳ it; yō shalbe an
inheritor of such riches as nither the covetous shall withdrawe from you, neyther the
thefe shall steale, neither yet yᵉ mothe cor-
rupte. Dissyre sistʳ to understand yᵉ law of
yᵉ lord yoʳ god. Lyve styll to dey, yᵗ yō
by deth may purches eternell lyfe; or after yoʳ
deth enioye the lyfe purchessed yoʷ by Christis
death, and trust not yᵗ yᵉ tenderness of yoʳ age
shall lengthen yoʳ life: for assone, if god will,
goith yᵉ young as the old; and laboure alway
to lerne to dey. Deney yᵉ world, difey yᵉ devall,
and dispyse yᵉ flesh. Delite yoʳ selfe onely in
yᵉ lord. Be penitent for yoʳ syns, and yet
despayre not. Be steady in faythe yet p̃sume
not, and desyre with S. Pawle to be desolvid
and to be with Xᵗ with whom even in death
there is lyfe. Be lyke the good servant, and
even at midnight be wakyng; least when death
comyth and stealythe upon yō lyke a thefe in
yᵉ night yoᵘ be with the evel servant found
slepinge, and least for lacke of oyle ye be
found lyk the first foulsh wence, and lyke him

that had not on the wedyng garment and thẽ be cast out from the marriage.   Risyst in ye, as I trust ye do, and seeing ye have yᵉ name of a cristian, as neare as ye can folowe the stepes of yoʳ master Chst, and take up yoʳ crosse; lay yoʳ syns on his backe, and always embrace him; and as towchynge my dethe reioyce as I do, and adsist yᵗ I shalbe delyvred of yᵉ corruption and put on incorruption, for I am assurede yᵗ I shall for losyng of a mortall lyfe finde an imortall felisity.   Pray God graunt yō send yō of his grace to lyve in his feare, and to dey in yᵉ love of ioy to you when the   shall arrive, neither for loue of lyfe nor feares of deathe. For if ye deney his truth to leg̃then yur life, God will deney yō and shorten yoʳ dayes; and if yō will cleaue to him, he will p̃long yoʳ days to yoʳ c̃ōfort and his glory, to the wch glory, God beinge minde and yō herafter, when it shall please God to call yō.   Farewell good systʳ put yoʳ onely trust in God, who onely must uphold yō yoʳ loving syst.

JANE DUDLEY "

A LETTER-FROM LADY JANE DUDLEY TO HER FATHER, THE
DUKE OF SUFFOLK, WRITTEN FROM THE TOWER A FEW
WEEKS BEFORE HER DEATH.

This letter is taken from a copy in Harleian MSS. 2194. f. 23.ᵇ In which
it is introduced by the following remark.

This duke's facility, too, by practises, had occasioned
the troubles wᵗʰ wᶜʰ this realme had for some yeares beene
distractede, and his rash ingratitude (the queene havenge
once pardoned him beyond expectation) had diverted the
current of the queenes clemency towards his daughter the
Lady Jane, whose life (yt was generally conceived) shee
would have pardoned, but her father's miscouncelled rash-
nes hastened her death. A little before wᶜʰ shee sent unto
him this letter followinge:

Father, although it hath pleased God to
hasten my death by you, by whom my life should
rather have been lengthened, yet I can so patient-
ly take it, that I yield God more hearty thanks
for shortening my woful days, than if all the
world had been given into my possession, with
life lengthened at my own will. And albeit I am
very well assured of your impatient dolours, re-
doubled many ways, both in bewailing your own
woe, and especially, as I am informed, my woful estate: yet my dear father, if I may, without
offence, rejoice in my own mishaps, herein I may
account myself blessed, that washing my hands
with the innocence of my fact, my guiltless blood
may cry before the Lord, Mercy to the innocent!

And yet though I must needs acknowledge, that being constrained, and as you know well enough continually assayed, yet in taking upon me, I seemed to consent, and therein greviously offended the queen and her laws, yet do I assuredly trust that this my offence towards God is so much the less, in that being in so royal estate as I was, my enforced honour never mingled with mine innocent heart. And thus, good father, I have opened unto you the state wherein I presently stand, my death at hand, although to you perhaps it may seem woful, yet to me there is nothing that can be more welcome than from this vale of misery to aspire to that heavenly throne of all joy and pleasure, with Christ my Saviour: in whose steadfast faith, (if it may be lawful for the daughter so to write to the father) the Lord that hath hitherto strengthened you, so continue to keep you, that at the last we may meet in heaven with the Father, Son, and Holy Ghost.

I am,

Your obedient daughter till death,

JANE DUDLEY.

A PRAYER COMPOSED BY LADY JANE DUDLEY SHORTLY
BEFORE HER EXECUTION.

O Lord, thou God and father of my life! hear me, poor and desolate woman, which flyeth unto thee only, in all troubles and miseries. Thou, O Lord, art the only defender and deliverer of those that put their trust in thee; and, therefore, I, being defiled with sin, encumbered with affliction, unquieted with troubles, wrapped in cares, overwhelmed with miseries, vexed with temptations, and grievously tormented with the long imprisonment of this vile mass of clay, my sinful body, do come unto thee, O merciful Saviour, craving thy mercy and help, without the which so little hope of deliverance is left, that I may utterly despair of my liberty. Albeit, it is expedient, that seeing our life standeth upon trying, we should be visited some time with some adversity, whereby we might both be tried whether we be of thy flock or no; and also know thee and ourselves the better; yet thou that saidst thou wouldst not suffer us to be tempted above our power, be merciful unto me, now a miserable wretch, I beseech thee; which, with Solomon, do cry unto thee, humbly desiring thee, that I may neither be too much puffed up with prosperity, neither too much depressed with adversity; lest I,

being too full, should deny thee, my God; or being
too low brought, should despair and blaspheme thee,
my Lord and Saviour. O merciful God, consider
my misery, best known unto thee; and be thou now
unto me a strong tower of defence, I humbly require thee. Suffer me not to be tempted above
my power, but either be thou a deliverer unto me
out of this great misery, or else give me grace pa-
tiently to bear thy heavy hand and sharp correction.
It was thy right hand that delivered the people
of Israel out of the hands of Pharaoh, which for
the space of four hundred years did oppress them,
and keep them in bondage; let it therefore likewise seem good to thy fatherly goodness, to deliver me, sorrowful wretch, for whom thy son
Christ shed his precious blood on the cross, out
of this miserable captivity and bondage, wherein
I am now. How long wilt thou be absent?—for
ever? Oh, Lord! hast thou forgotten to be gracious,
and hast thou shut up thy loving kindness in
displeasure? wilt thou be no more entreated? Is
thy mercy clear gone for ever, and thy promise
come utterly to an end for evermore? why dost
thou make so long tarrying? shall I despair of
thy mercy? Oh God! far be that from me; I am
thy workmanship, created in Christ Jesus; give
me grace therefore to tarry thy leisure, and pa-
tiently to bear thy works, assuredly knowing,

that as thou canst, so thou wilt deliver me, when
it shall please thee, nothing doubting or mistrust-
ing thy goodness towards me; for thou knowest
better what is good for me than I do; therefore
do with me in all things what thou wilt, and
plague me what way thou wilt. Only, in the mean
time, arm me, I beseech thee, with thy armour,
that I may stand fast, my loins being girded about
with verity, having on the breast-plate of righteousness, and shod with the shoes prepared by the
gospel of peace; above all things, taking to me the
shield of faith, wherewith I may be able to quench
all the fiery darts of the wicked; and taking the
helmet of salvation, and the sword of thy spirit,
which is thy most holy word; praying always,
with all manner of prayer and supplication, that I
may refer myself wholly to thy will, abiding thy
pleasure, and comforting myself in those troubles
that it shall please thee to send me; seeing such
troubles be profitable for me, and seeing I am
assuredly persuaded that it cannot but be well all
thou doest. Hear me, O merciful Father, for his
sake, whom thou wouldest should be a sacrifice
for my sins; to whom with thee and the Holy
Ghost, be all honour and glory. Amen!

LADY JANE DUDLEY'S SPEECH ON THE SCAFFOLD.

My lords, and you good christian people,
which come to see me die, I am under a law, and
by that law, as a never erring judge, I am condemned to die, not for any thing I have offended
the Queen's Majesty, for I will wash my hands
guiltless thereof, and deliver to my God a soul as
pure from such trespass, as innocence from injustice ; but only for that I consented to the thing
which I was enforced unto, constraint making
the law believe I did that which I never understood.
Notwithstanding, I have offended Almighty God in
that I have followed over-much the lust of mine
own flesh, and the pleasures of this wretched world,
neither have I lived according to the knowledge
that God hath given me, for which cause God hath
appointed unto me this kind of death, and that most
worthily, according to my deserts; how be it, I
thank him heartily that he hath given me time to
repent my sins here in this world, and to reconcile
myself to my redeemer, whom my former vanities
have in a great measure displeased.   Wherefore,
my lords, and all you good christian people, I
must earnestly desire you all to pray with and for
me whilst I am yet alive, that God of his infinite
goodness and mercy will forgive me my sins, how
numberless and grievous soever against him : and

I beseech you all to bear me witness that I here
die a true christian woman, professing and avouch-
ing from my soul that I trust to be saved by the
blood, passion, and merits of Jesus Christ my
Saviour only, and by none other means; casting
far behind me all the works and merits of mine
own actions, as things so far short of the true duty
I owe, that I quake to think how much they may
stand up against me. And now, I pray you all
pray for me, and with me.

In a small manuscript on vellum, in the Harleian collection[a] in the British Museum, containing a Manual of Prayers, which is considered to have originally belonged "to some English Protestant of quality, who was cast into prison wrongfully, according to his own opinion;" but was afterwards used both by Lady Jane and her husband, Lord Guildford Dudley, when in the Tower; these illustrious persons wrote the following passages, and which render this little volume perhaps the most interesting relic of misfortunes which is extant. It is about four inches long, nearly two inches in thickness, and contains thirty-five Prayers: as from its size, there is but a very small margin,

---

[a] Harl. MSS. No. 2342.

As an account of the contents of this valuable MS. must be deemed of much interest, from the circumstance of its having been used in the devotions of Lady Jane Grey, the following is extracted from the Harleian Catalogue.

A prayer for patience in Tribulation as Christ was patient f. 1
A prayer conserninge the love of my neighbour 5
A prayer for forgiveness of sins; wherein gloteny is
    added to lechery............................ 9
A prayer for our Enemyse 15
For pacyens in Tribulation 15ᵇ
For true wisdom 16
A confession of sins to God, seeming to want the begin-
    ning; here, among other sins, the penitent
    chargeth himself with adulterie and theft....... 18
'A praier to our Lord Jeshu Christ, in which he desires
    grace pacyently to suffer..................... 21ᵇ
The praier of Quene Ester for help agaynst her enymyes 27ᵇ

not more than three lines of the passages alluded to occur
on the same leaf; they are written at the bottom of the

The prāer of Sara the daughter of Raguell whan she was
    slaundred 28ᵇ
The praier of Judath for the victorie of Olyfuernes.....29
The praier of Jessus the sonne of Sirake..............29ᵇ
The praier of the three children that were delyuered
    from the hote burnying fire............... ..32
The praier of Manasseth, King of Juda..............35ᵇ
A prayer for grace to believe and trust in Jesus Christ. 38
A prayer for assistance against many of the author's in
    firmities: amongst other sins he mentions "Pol-
    linge of poore people, and crabbedness agaynst
    those that were with him in howseholde".......39
A prayer to the blessed trenyte.....................42ᵇ
A prayer to God for delyuerance from the power of all
    his enemyes, and frome all theym that consented
    to his destructyon and pardicione.............44
A prayer against the temptations of the flesshe, the worlde
    and the deuylle............................45ᵇ
A peticyon or prayer for [i. e. *against*] all the evylles of
    paynes and punishments 48ᵇ
A deuoute prayer to Criste the seconde person in trynyte,
    our onely redemer, God and man 49ᵇ
A peticion aud praier to our lorde for delyuerance from
    his enemys 59ᵇ
Ejaculations collected from the Psalms and other Scrip-
    tures, beseeching the divine assistance in the
    author's extreme misery....................62
The songe of Austeyn and Ambrose 74ᵇ
Saynt Jerom's deuocion oute of Dauyd's Saulter 77ᵇ

page, and are continued on the opposite and following
ones. The manuscript which is bound in red morocco and
ornamented, was once "illuminated by some foreigner,
but has since been abused, and is now imperfect in
two places;" with this exception, however, it is in fine
preservation, and callous indeed must be the person who
can turn over its pages with indifference. The compiler
of the Harleian Catalogue, conjectures that it was written
for the use of Edward Seymour, Duke of Somerset, the
Protector, "upon his first commitment to the Tower of
London, and that the last five prayers were added after his
second commitment, which ended in his execution; but if it
were so, 'tis easy to apprehend how it might come into the
hands of that noble, but unfortunate lady, the Lady Jane
Grey." However probable the conjecture may be, that the
volume once belonged to the Protector, it does not appear to
be supported by the least evidence; and though Lady Ka-

A praier to the Father..............................106[b]
A praier to the Holy Goste........................107
A praier to the Trenyte............................107[b]
A praier to Jesu Christe 108
The Lord's prayer, followed by many holy ejaculations. 109[b]
　　These are suitable to the condition of a person in tribu-
　　　lation: yet some of them do seem to import a
　　　deliverance.
　　　　　Now follow, by another hand,
A prayer in Trobil................................137
A prayer for the lyghtenyng of the Holye Ghoste 138
A prayer in aduersitte and greuous distresse
A prayer for strengthe of mynde to beare the Crosse..140
A prayer of the faythful person in adversite 143

therine Grey, the sister of Lady Jane, married Edward
Seymour, the Duke's son, that alliance did not take place
till some years after Lady Jane's execution; hence the book,
if it once belonged to the Protector, is not likely to have
fallen into her possession: but as her husband's brother
John, Earl of Warwick, married Anne Seymour, the daughter of that celebrated statesman, it is highly probable that it
was given to Lord Guildford by his sister-in-law, after he
became a prisoner, and if this conjecture be correct, the
similarity between his situation, and that of its former owner,
must have rendered it a most appropriate present.

The note which first occurs was written by Lord
Guildford Dudley; it was evidently addressed to his wife's
father, the Duke of Suffolk; and, as has been before sur-
mised, in all probability the book having been occasionally
borrowed by each of the unfortunate prisoners, as no other
method of communication was perhaps permitted, it was
made the means of conveying those assurances of duty and
affection, which have almost consecrated its pages.

Your louyng and obedyent son wischethe unto
your grace long lyfe in this world, with as muche
joye and comforte, as euer I wyshte to my selfe;
and in the world to come joy euerlasting. Your
most humble son tel his dethe,   G. Duddeley.

Some pages further on, Lady Jane Grey addressed her
father in the following manner.

The Lorde comforte your grace, and that in
his worde whearein all creatures onlye are to be
comforted.   And thoughe it hath pleased God to

I

take awaye 2 of your children: yet thincke not, I
most humblye beseech youre grace, that you haue
loste them; but truste that we, by leafinge this
mortall life, haue wunne an immortal life.　And I,
for my parte, as I haue honoured your grace in this
life, wyll praye for you in another life.　Youre
gracys humble daughter, JANE DUDDELEY.

　, The ensuing passage in Lady Jaae Grey's autograph,
was written at the request of Sir John Brydges, the Lieutenant of the Tower, who being solicitous to obtain a
memorial of his prisoners, is said to have requested her to
write some lines in it, he in all probability having obtained
a promise thar the volume should be given to him after her
decease.　But Mr. Howard asserts, that "between the an-
nouncement of the fatal order for execution and its fulfilment,
the Lieutenant of the Tower, evidently impressed with love
and respect for the unhappy sufferers, was anxious to procure some memorial of his prisoners, and accordingly he
presented to them the manual of devotions in question;" he,
however, afterwards suggests that they had borrowed the
book.　In a former part of these remarks, another conjecture
on the manner in which it fell into Lady Jane's hands has
been submitted, but it would be useless to pursue the enquiry;
especially as some observations connected with the subject
will be found in the memoir in this volume.

　　Forasmuche as you haue desired so simple a
woman to wrighte in so worthy a booke, gode
mayster Lieufenante therefore I shalle as a frende,
desyre you, and as a christian require you, to call
vpyon God, to encline youre harte to his lawes, to

quicken you in his waye, and not to take the worde of trewethe vtterlye oute of youre mouthe. Lyue styll to dye, that by deathe you may purchase eternall life; and remember howe the ende of Mathusael, whoe as we reade in the scriptures, was the longeste liuer that was of a manne, died at the laste. For, as the Precher sayethe, there is a tyme to be borne, and a tyme to dye; and the daye of deathe is better than the daye of oure birthe. Youres, as the Lorde knowethe, as a frende,

JANE DUDDELBY.

The following lines are said to have been written by
Lady Jane Grey on the walls of her apartment in the Tower,
with a pin; but it is to be observed, that though numerous
devices inscribed by the unfortunate persons who have at
different times been the inhabitants of that fortress, were
discovered on making some alterations a few years ago,
and the whole of which are inserted in the XIII Volume of
the *Archæologia*, not the slightest remains of these verses
were to be found. As this circumstance does not however
prove that they never existed, and as they have been constantly attributed to Lady Jane Grey, they could not with
propriety be omitted in a collection of her writings; whilst
the question of their authenticity is of course left to the
sagacity of the reader.

Non aliena putes homini quæ obtingere possunt,
Sors hodierna mihi, cras erit illa tibi!

Which has been thus translated:
     To mortals' common fate thy mind resign,
     My lot to day, to-morrow may be thine.
Also, thus:
     Think not, O mortal! vainly gay,
     That thou from human woes art free;
     The bitter cup I drink to day,
     To-morrow, may be drank by thee.

The following are also said to have been written in a
similar manner.

Deo juvante, nil nocet livor malus;
Et non juvante, nil juvat labor gravis:
         Post tenebras, spero lucem.

Whilst God assists us, envy bites in vain,
If God forsake us, fruitless all our pain—
      I hope for light after the darkness.

A more elegant translation which has appeared, is,

Harmless all malice, if our God be nigh :
Fruitless all pains, if he his help deny.
Patient I pass these gloomy hours away,
And wait the morning of eternal day!

THE END.

Johnson, Typ. Brook Street, Holborn.

CPSIA information can be obtained at www.ICGtesting.com
Printed in the USA
BVOW01s2348170215

388204BV00015B/154/P